Conquer Your Closing:
Insider Secrets for Today's Savvy Home Buyer

Karen Simpson-Hankins

Conquer Your Closing:

Insider Secrets for Today's Savvy Home Buyer

Karen Simpson-Hankins

K Hankins 2014

Blue Elephant Press

Raleigh, NC

For permission requests, please contact the author directly at:

Karen Simpson-Hankins

permission@KarenSimpsonHankins.com

http://www.KarenSimpsonHankins.com

Published by:

Blue Elephant Press

info@blueelephantpress.com

www.blueelephantpress.com

This book is dedicated to . . .

all of my clients and industry partners ~

you have been such a huge part of my career and life.

and to my family ~

thank you for supporting me and believing in me through countless hours of work and dedication to my clients.

I am very blessed and I love you all.

Praise for Karen Simpson-Hankins

"I have known Karen for over 30 years. She is honest, hardworking and does her best for all of her customers and clients."

~ Bill Porter / Realtor

"Karen always put my client's interests ahead of her own. It was never about how much money she could make brokering a loan. It was always 'what is the best possible product I can deliver for this person at the best possible price to them.' She saved my clients thousands of dollars over the years with her vast knowledge of the financing world."

~ Mark Rieger / Realtor

"As a Manager for a top lender in Oregon, I had the pleasure of working with Karen on hundreds of files over approximately eight years. Due to the quality, accuracy and her concern for customer care, I always felt that her clients were very lucky to have her as their mortgage loan broker. Her knowledge of industry and investor requirements allowed her to guide her clients on a personal level and "custom fit" their individual needs in price, benefits and products."

~ Sandra K. Jones / VP and Retail Lending Manager

"Karen is a very knowledgeable person. She knows her job and does it well, going above and beyond expectation. She was my mortgage broker; she helped me structure my construction project which saved me thousands of dollars. I am so blessed to know her, have her as my neighbor and best of all, to be my good friend."

~ Penni St .Pierre / Client

"Karen is one of the best Mortgage Brokers that I have worked with in my 28-year escrow career. Organized, prepared, helpful, friendly, efficient, can-do attitude—

Karen has all of the best skills and updated mortgage information that work for our mutual clients without charging exorbitant fees. She is most professional and a pleasure to work with."

~ Patty Yancey / Branch Manager and Senior Certified Escrow Officer

"In over 30 years of real estate practice, the one guaranteed tool in my repertoire to ensure success of any given deal was Karen. Whether it was a Federal VA transaction, FHA or conventional loan, it never mattered. If she told me she could do it, the loan was as good as done. And more reassuring than the sale was the fact that my buyers always migrated back to her for refinancing needs as a matter of professional capacity, trust, competence and results—whether I was involved or not! Karen gives new meaning to the word client."

~ Walt Reuber / Realtor

"In the roller coaster world of real estate, one thing I found that did not change was the ever constant Karen Simpson-Hankins. With her vast knowledge of the mortgage industry, she provided a service to her clientele that was beyond compare. From beginning to end, she was there for her customer finding the perfect product that would best fit their needs. Her attention to detail and her genuine concern for her client earned her the biggest compliment—repeat business from the customers that became her friends. I had the privilege to work with her as the escrow officer on numerous transactions over the years."

~ Kim Hicks / Escrow Officer

"The knowledge that Karen possesses when it comes to home mortgages is like a breath of fresh air! From start to finish, she took all the worry out of refinancing our home. She explains each step of the way in a clear, concise manner. Her knowledge and expertise coupled with an honest and ethical background, gives kudos to the mortgage business! Thanks for a job well done Karen!"

~ Gail Wood / Client

Contents

Introduction

IT IS A FACT . . . many people will fail to get the best deal possible when shopping for a home loan.

This is primarily because they don't know the proper questions to ask lenders, real estate professionals, and other individuals they work with throughout this process.

How are we going to change this fact with one book?

In preparing to write this book, I spent months looking at other competitive mortgage books on the market. Personally, I found them to be too technical, dry and difficult to understand. And more importantly, there always seemed to be one very critical element missing—YOU, the mortgage buyer. These books simply failed to tell you what you really need to know.

This is why I have designed my book in a very consumer friendly format. I want it to be a resource that goes with you during visits with lenders. As such, I've included checklists and sample forms inside that you can use to compare lender's rates, fees, and products. I want you to be assured that you're comparing apples to apples and getting all of the important questions answered during this process.

You may find this book relatively short when compared to the others on the market. This is because I have removed all of the theory and technical jargon. You don't need it. I filled this book only with the most vital details you need to know in order to accomplish your goal.

This book is not based on the technical aspects of each loan product, but on what's most important to YOU—how to save time, money and stress while shopping for and closing on your Best Fit Mortgage™.

It's my objective to help you become as knowledgeable as possible before you go house hunting, shopping for that mysterious mortgage, or signing on the dotted line.

Whether you're securing a first mortgage, looking to refinance an existing mortgage, interested in building your dream home or pulling out some equity for home improvements, this book will tell you what you need to know. I show you:

- All the correct questions to ask potential lenders
- What supportive documentation you need to give your lender
- How to negotiate and lock-in the lowest interest rate
- How to save money on closing costs to ensure confidence that your loan is the best fit for long-term financial health

Obtaining a mortgage can impact all of your financial goals and I want to help ensure that your new home loan fits comfortably into all areas of your life.

I understand that it's not just a house; it's your home and one of the biggest investments that you'll make throughout your lifetime. When we are finished, my hope is that you're going to feel like you've just had coffee with a very good friend.

Why would you listen to me?

The purpose of this book—and for that matter my entire 37-year career as a mortgage professional—has been to help individuals navigate the world of mortgage finance as an educated consumer.

I wanted to help them (and now YOU) avoid the mistakes most consumers make in the loan process that can be expensive and devastating to their financial future. These are the mistakes that can affect your life for years to come.

I am confident that you will find the information contained here to be a very powerful financial tool in your home-buying arsenal as well. And I want to thank you for purchasing it.

I have been a Mortgage Broker / Banker / Home Loan Consultant for over thirty-seven years. My reputation has always been one of working to "custom fit" a home loan to my client's individual needs. This Best Fit Mortgage™ process also allowed me to provide superior customer service, affordable pricing, and strong attention to detail. My clients have always described this method as a 'virtually stress-free home buying experience.'

I worked for several mortgage companies throughout my career and launched my own successful company in 2001 until my retirement in 2011.

As a licensed mortgage broker in the state of Oregon, my mission was to provide a higher level of consumer awareness around the biggest mortgage mistakes consumers make and teach them how to save time, money and stress in the process.

My business has always been a 100% referral base, as I have been blessed with many lifelong friendships of Realtors® and clients. Over the years, I have provided thousands of home loans, saving thousands in the process by finding the best product for each client.

As an approved trainer for the Oregon Real Estate Division, I have also been providing workshops and continuing education for Realtors® and consumers for more than 30 years.

With a background in originating, processing, underwriting and closing home loans, my expertise has benefited thousands of homebuyers in my local market and throughout the state of Oregon. And now, it's time this knowledge benefitted YOU.

Surviving the Credit Crisis

OVER THE PAST FEW YEARS 'the housing bubble,' 'the mortgage credit crisis' and the collapse of the 'subprime market,' has had a tremendous impact on our overall economy.

Foreclosures are at levels never before seen in the mortgage industry. Thousands of families are struggling to keep their homes amidst rising unemployment rates, soft markets, deflated property values and the excessive tightening of mortgage guidelines. This is making it almost impossible for some individuals to sell, purchase or refinance a home.

People are taking on second jobs, overtime when available and depleting their savings or retirement accounts just to survive.

How did it happen?

There's a lot of speculation and finger pointing going on, but primarily, it's because the housing industry got greedy. Yes, I believe that not one area of the market is to blame, but the **entire industry**.

Lenders, real estate professionals, appraisers, mortgage brokers, investors, builders, consumers and the secondary market giants—Fannie Mae (FNMA) and Freddie Mac (FHLMC)—all played a part in the collapse of our housing industry across the country.

In the past, banks would make home loans and keep them until they were paid off. Strict underwriting guidelines were used to ensure quality and limited risk to the lender. If something went wrong with a loan, the bank was responsible and they would lose money.

As demand grew, things changed. Banks and mortgage lenders began to originate home loans and immediately resell them in the form of mortgage-backed securities on the secondary market (i.e. Wall Street). This allowed banks and lenders to pass any potential risk on to investors. It also renewed their funding sources, so they could lend to even more borrowers. Guidelines began to loosen, which resulted in more lenient underwriting, less concern for overall risk and the development of more aggressive financing products. It was all about supply and demand . . . and there were both!

The flood gates opened and banks were originating home loans from many different channels—both retail and wholesale by utilizing mortgage brokers and correspondent lenders—with not much concern. The loans were packaged and sold in bulk as securities, so it didn't matter if a few loans defaulted because overall the investments were performing . . . at least for a while.

The various political sectors would have the public believe that the entire blame of fault lies with greedy independent mortgage brokers. They say the brokers were putting people into specialty loan products which provided the broker with the highest commission despite the affect the loans had on the consumer.

I'm sure that in some cases, as with any retail/commission-based industry, this was true. But as a veteran mortgage professional, I personally take offense to the accusations that we were all knowingly taking advantage of the consumer just because we wanted higher commissions for ourselves.

The banks, mortgage companies and their various investors created those specialty products to address each segment of the market in the first place, paying higher commissions on those products to entice mortgage brokers to sell them. It was big business in the housing and subprime markets and everyone wanted their piece of the "American Dream Pie."

The subprime market was a term used to define higher risk borrowers. It usually consisted of borrowers that could not prove their income, had lower credit scores due to previous credit problems or were providing small down payments on high-risk properties.

Lenders and their investors—those who purchased these types of loans after they closed on the secondary market—loved them because they could charge higher rates, bigger fees and set pretty much any terms they wanted because high risk borrowers have fewer options available to them.

These type of loans usually consisted of:

- **Short loan terms:** the loan usually had a term of 2–5 years. Some loans had longer terms, but with the potential of huge interest rate increases after the initial fixed payment term.
- **Adjustable rate loans:** loans where the interest rate can change on a pre-determined basis.
- **High loan to value ratios:** loans that were a zero down option loan or that were as high as 100–125% of the appraised value.
- **High loan origination fees:** usually 1–5% of the loan amount.
- **Large pre-payment penalties:** a penalty if the loan was paid off or refinanced in the first five years.
- **Teaser rates, with negative amortization:** low, unrealistic rates that were guaranteed to go up within the first few years of the loan

term and a minimum required payment that did not cover the interest due, so the unpaid balance continued to grow.

When the whole thing fell apart, all areas of the industry were refusing to take responsibility for their part in the collapse and looking for someone else to blame.

It's been called predatory lending, but is it?

It depends on your point of view. It's not predatory lending if you have an educated consumer making their financial decisions based on their ability to pay. But it could be considered predatory if the program guidelines were not disclosed in their entirety.

I know from personal experience that the home-buying process is an emotionally charged experience and consumers don't always make their financial decisions based on sound judgment when their "dream home" is involved.

As a broker, I chose not to participate with those specialty products that I felt were not good for the consumer. A lot of the negative amortization loans that had teaser rates (rates as low as 1%) were just too good to be true and too complicated for the average consumer to navigate.

My clients trusted that I was not going to put them in a loan product that was not right for them. I spent a lot of time making sure that my clients were well educated on their choices and encouraged them to keep asking questions until they found the home loan that was a best fit for them.

I've witnessed individuals with many years of experience in the real estate industry getting involved in the negative amortization products. They go in thinking they could sell an investment property before they got too far in debt and it has back-fired even on them.

So how was the average consumer supposed to thoroughly understand those products? I don't believe they were ever meant to!

The housing bubble burst, the slump hit and consumers couldn't sell their properties because they owed more than the current appraised value. This spelled disaster for everyone involved. So . . . what happened next?

Change, change and more change! Changes that were actually a reversion back to original lending guidelines from years past and new disclosures designed to protect us from ourselves. But all of this change never addressed the real issue. It only continues to muddy the water for consumers.

How do we begin to understand mortgage money today?

As we move forward into a new era of home lending, good credit, complete documentation and planning will be a requirement when obtaining a loan.

My mission in writing this book is to give consumers the education they need to make good, sound financial choices when borrowing for a home purchase, but still be able to enjoy the emotional element involved when making such a life changing decision.

In this book, I will show you:

- How mortgage brokers/lenders make money
- What questions you need to ask every lender
- Which closing costs are negotiable
- How to get the best value for your hard earned dollar

This book will teach you how to potentially save thousands of dollars in fees and interest on your next home loan, give you the confidence you need to survive the mortgage credit crisis, and provide tips to find a great deal while becoming a wiser, more educated consumer!

You are about to discover what most people will never know about having the ultimate mortgage experience. Let's get started.

The 4 Biggest Mortgage Mistakes (Almost) Every Consumer Makes

CHOOSING A LENDER by interest rate alone may seem like a wise-financial decision, but it's actually the first mistake consumers make in shopping for a mortgage.

The cost of your loan involves more than just interest. It includes loan fees, discount points—fees used to buy down the interest rate, and many other hidden costs or junk fees.

You need to compare all costs to see if a product is right for you and your financial goals. So let's discuss how to uncover the hidden costs that affect your loan.

When shopping, ask a mortgage broker or lender if they charge for items such as:

- A Processing Fee
- Administration Fee
- Wire Fees
- Courier Fees
- Document Preparation Fee

You will also have closing costs that consist of:

- Title Insurance
- Escrow or Attorney Fees
- Appraisal Fee
- Credit Report Fee
- Tax Service Fee
- Flood Determination Fee
- Recording Fees

These fees will vary depending on what state you live in, but they should not change much or at all from lender to lender.

Most wholesale lenders will charge an Underwriting Fee, which is typical but should not be excessive.

Remember when comparing different lenders that they are all utilizing the same services so there should not be much (if any) variation in these fees. If there is, consider it a red flag for that particular lender and question them on the variation.

Also ask every lender you speak with if the prices quoted are for a specific lock-in period. A lock-in period is where the lender guarantees a rate for a specific period of time. As an informed consumer, you want to be aware of any increases or changes in price as you move through the loan process.

In my career, I always quoted a lock-in period at thirty days to allow sufficient time to process the loan. I have noticed some lenders quoting these lock-in periods at ten days, which means the lender is not guaranteeing any rate until the loan is approved and within ten days of closing. It is simply a marketing tactic that makes their rates appear lower.

The second mistake is not asking about pre-payment penalties.

Some lenders may be advertising an interest rate that appears lower but is actually higher due to a prepayment penalty. This may not be an issue to you today, but if interest rates drop and you want to refinance or sell your home, this penalty will affect your payoff costs.

Be aware and don't accept loans with a prepayment penalty, they can be devastating when your financial situation changes through a refinancing or home sale.

I've seen large prepayment penalties that consisted of several thousand dollars placed in effect for up to 5 years. Make sure you always confirm in writing that your loan does not have a prepayment penalty prior to signing any final documents or contracts.

The third mistake consumers make is not shopping around or accepting a one-size-fits-all loan.

I personally feel that it is in every consumer's best interest to deal with a reputable, licensed mortgage broker. Seek out a company that has a multitude of lenders, not just a single source like most banks.

I've read a lot of negative comments about using a mortgage broker, all of which are nothing more than scare tactics. If you think about it, it only makes sense because a mortgage broker does not have any financial interest with a particular lender.

They can aggressively shop products for you without being limited to a single source or have concern over betraying their employer. They really are in a position to find the Best Fit Mortgage™ for you. This proved an incredible advantage for my clients over the past thirty-seven years.

Not all lenders see things in black and white. It's very much a what-makes-sense-for-my-client business. All lenders have their hot buttons—the financial areas where they may be more sensitive than others—depending on their investors and whether or not the loan is being sold on the secondary market to Fannie Mae or Freddie Mac.

As a broker, I was always aware of these hot buttons and I could direct my borrower to a lender that would best serve them. Even though all lenders work basically by the same set of rules, especially on conventional loans, there's always a certain amount of interpretation involved with each underwriter and their reaction can vary from lender to lender.

If one lender says "No," try and find out their reasons for denying the loan. Don't give up; continue to look for additional guidance from your broker on how to move forward. I always described this process to my clients like this:

> *"Processing a loan is like putting together a jigsaw puzzle and you don't know what the picture will look like until all of the pieces are in place."*

Ask questions and be completely forthcoming and honest with your mortgage professional. Most of them will do their very best to get you what you need. But . . . if you don't like the answers you receive, don't be afraid to go out and ask someone else!

I saw myself—the broker in the application process—as someone who really needed to listen to your whole story. If I didn't have all of the information, I couldn't do my job correctly. And in the end, it paid my clients well for me to be a very good listener—the result was incredible customer service and very few surprises in the loan process.

The fourth mistake consumers make is in doing nothing because they don't think they'll qualify.

As a mortgage professional, I had access to a lot programs. Even if your credit is less than perfect, there may be a competitive program that can help you realize your dreams.

As a consumer, it is worth the time to do some quick research into your own credit worthiness, discover any weak areas, and get to work on improving your overall borrowing power. You may not be ready to buy today, but have a plan so that you will be ready six months, one year, or even two years down the road. Just don't give up!

What Can You Really Afford?

DID YOU KNOW that it's your responsibility to determine what mortgage you can afford? It's true. Here are a few questions I would ask a new client sitting at my desk:

- How much do you feel that you can afford?
- Have you thought about what monthly payment would feel comfortable to you?
- Have you calculated your other monthly expenses?

I can't tell you how many times I've asked those three questions in the last thirty-seven years. And far too many times the client just looked at me with a blank stare and said, "*I don't know . . . that's what I thought you were going to tell me?*"

I would follow up with another question. "*Are you currently paying rent?*"

The client would then say something like, "*Well, I'm paying $800 a month, but I think I can pay more.*"

Again I would ask, "*Do you know what your total out-of-pocket expenses are per month? Expenses like car payments, credit card payments, student loans, food, clothing, gas, entertainment, gifts and day-care. I can tell you what the lender will be willing to lend based on your gross monthly income and your consumer debt, but that doesn't really take your other expenses into consideration."*

These expenses are part of your monthly responsibility and directly affect the level of financial comfort you will enjoy as a home owner. The lender cannot determine that for you.

Let's go over an example: The lender says you're approved for a $250,000 mortgage. That means that $250,000 is the maximum amount a lender would be willing to lend to you for a mortgage. The question here is: can you afford that mortgage? The answer is not necessarily YES as it depends on your overall financial picture and spending habits.

Here's how the loan process works: An underwriter who never speaks with you will look at your application including your income level, assets, job security, consumer debt and all of the supporting documentation that has been compiled.

They will run that information through an electronic approval process and obtain an approval, denial or caution based on the information that has been presented to them. This is where the lender determines your maximum loan amount.

Not only is it vitally important that all of your financial information be presented, it is also very important how well the mortgage broker documents this information for the lender.

This is the reason for making sure you give your mortgage broker or lender all of your financial information, because if your file is incomplete, it may result in your loan application coming back denied.

However, before this process ever takes place, the responsibility falls back to you in knowing what monthly payment you can comfortably afford. The electronic approval process the underwriter is using cannot determine this factor for you. To provide you some assistance, I've included a worksheet in this chapter to help in determining your actual monthly expenses.

There is nothing more frustrating than finding out you won't be able to go on vacation because your "dream home" has just eaten up your entire budget and there's no money left for fun.

It may be your dream home and you may love it, but the "new" wears off very quickly when you can't afford to do anything else. This can also be very tough on personal relationships.

The secret to all of this lies in your ability to make logical, unemotional decisions. You must approach this in a business-like manner because when people make decisions based on emotion, they tend to make mistakes.

Ask yourself these questions:

- How long do you plan on living in this new home?
- How long did you live in your last home?
- Are you expecting any major life changes such as new babies, elderly parents, retirement, relationship issues, or health concerns that may be a factor?
- When will your children be moving out?
- Are you going to need funds for their college education?
- Are you expecting a job promotion or possibly a job transfer?
- How is your overall job stability?
- If you do move in the future, will you keep this home as an investment / rental property or will you need to sell it?

- Is this a second home or vacation home?
- Can you afford upkeep and maintenance on two homes or will you need to rent it when you're not using it?
- What about the neighborhood? Are there any zoning issues?
- Does the overall condition of the neighborhood seem to be improving or deteriorating?
- Is there evidence of any city or county issues that may affect the livability or salability of your home? For example, a new bypass being considered, new airport, annexation or anything with commercial impact?
- Will you need to budget funds for repairs?
- Are there any environmental issues, possible drainage problems, or anything else of that nature?

These are the types of questions that need to be answered to insure you are making a sound business decision and not letting the emotions fueled by an incredible gourmet kitchen or jetted spa make the decision for you . . . a choice that you may regret later.

For first-time home buyers, it is extremely important that you take into consideration all of the "proposed" expenses that come along with home ownership as well. Expenses like . . .

- Increased utilities
- Property taxes
- Homeowner's insurance
- Maintenance and repairs
- Subdivision or PUD (Planned Unit Development) monthly dues,

which can be very expensive if there are a lot of amenities such as lawn care, pools, or recreation facilities

- Allowing a savings or emergency fund for unexpected expenses

The good news is, you do not have to account for every penny. At the very least, track your expenses for two or three months to get an accurate feel for what you really spend. Most of the clients who walked into my office had no idea.

When people examine their personal spending, they are usually shocked with their overall spending habits and how little they actually save. A common question I am asked is "*How much should I be saving*?"

It really depends on your overall financial goals, but most people should save at least 10 percent of their gross (before tax) income. It's important to pay yourself first, that way you're more likely to save on a regular basis.

You will probably need to revise your spending habits to allow for the increased expenses that come with home ownership. Where you decide to make cuts in your budget is a personal choice, but here are some ways that can help.

- **Reduce or eliminate consumer credit whenever possible:** credit cards, auto loans and other types of consumer credit can dangerously affect your overall financial wealth. Buying now and paying later encourages you to live beyond your means, and the interest rates on consumer debt are high, making it extremely difficult to pay back, especially, if you're only making the minimum required payment.

- **Avoid luxury spending:** most individuals today spend a great deal of money on luxury and non-essential items. Take a moment before you purchase an item and ask yourself, "*Do I really need this?*"

- **Buy essential items in bulk:** most items are less expensive when you buy them in larger-sized packaging or if bought in bulk. Also watch for sales and stock up on items you know you'll use on a continued basis, but always compare prices.
- **Research more expensive products before buying:** great quality doesn't always mean it has to cost more. Shop around and make sure that you are getting a good value before you buy. Especially, when it comes to electronics and gadgets. Also find out what kind of warranty is available, it can save you repair and maintenance costs down the road.

Most people borrow money to purchase something they can't afford to pay for in a lump sum with cash. This usually consists of items like homes, autos and college degrees. When used properly, debt can be a very valuable tool in achieving your financial goals and can even earn you additional money over time.

It's important to understand how the debt process works when it comes to determining what you qualify to borrow. Here is an example of the calculations that the lender will use in this process. This example does not take into consideration the different product types or down payment options, but just reflects the necessary qualifying ratios.

This particular example reflects a sales price of $125,000 combined with a 20% down payment, which equals a $100,000 loan on a 30-year fixed rate term (conventional loan) at an interest rate of 6.00%

Principle and interest payment: $599.55

Property taxes (1% = $1,250/per year divided by 12): $104.17

Home Insurance (0.5% = $625/per year divided by 12): $52.08

Total monthly PITI payment (principle, interest, taxes and insurance) now stands at $755.80.

Then total monthly consumer debt expenses are added: $450.00

(This includes things such as car loans, credit cards, student loans, etc.)

The total monthly out of pocket expense equals: $1,205.80

When qualifying, a lender will use what is called a front end ratio (PITI payment) of 28%, and a total debt ratio (total monthly expenses, including house payment) of 36%. Each of these numbers represents a percentage of your gross monthly income.

These 28/36 ratios are default ratios and will vary from program to program. Some loan programs will allow more lenient ratios, sometimes as high as 45%. But I do not recommend pushing these ratios to the maximum allowed, unless your spending habits support it and you have adequate residual income—the amount remaining to live on after paying your monthly obligations—left over to meet your lifestyle.

To continue with our example, we will base our qualification on an annual income of $40,000. The monthly gross (pre-tax) income used for qualifying would be $3,333.33 per month.

Our front end ratio (PITI) calculated at *($755.80 divided into $3,333.33)* would be at 22.7%. The total debt ratio *($1,205.80 divided into $3,333.33)* would be 36.2%. Both of these are within acceptable guidelines, but you need to remember that this is pre-tax income and doesn't actually reflect take home pay and residual cash.

Also, if your down payment is less than 20% of the sales price or appraised value of the home, the lender will require Private Mortgage Insurance (PMI) to be paid. This is typically charged as a monthly addition to your PITI payment. PMI requirements will vary depending on the loan product. Some can be very expensive, adding as much as $100.00 or more to your monthly payment depending on the PMI factor used. We will discuss PMI in more detail in a later chapter. But for now, know that it is one more monthly cost that could add up.

That's why it's incredibly important for you to calculate ALL of your expenses to know if this will be a comfortable, affordable payment for YOU!

For more information on calculating qualifying ratios, go to my website at www.karensimpsonhankins.com and click on the Mortgage Calculators under the Resources section. You will find several tools on the website or you can use the following calculations to help determine your loan qualification and affordability.

Calculating Your Maximum Mortgage

To compute your maximum mortgage amount for a loan, you must use the lenders qualifying ratios for your particular loan. But for our example, let's continue using the default ratios of 28/36.

HOUSING EXPENSE RATIO

Total Gross Monthly Income: $_______________ x 0.28

(your gross monthly income times 28 percent)

Maximum allowed PITI plus any HOA fees: $____________ (1)

(principle, interest, taxes, insurance plus Homeowner Association fees)

TOTAL DEBT RATIO

Total Gross Monthly Income: $_______________ x 0.36

(your gross monthly income times 36 percent)

Maximum allowed for PITI + HOA fees and other monthly debts:
$_______________

Minus total monthly debt payments: $_______________

Maximum allowed for PITI + HOA fees: $_____________ (2)

Choose the lower of (1) or (2): $_____________

This figure represents the maximum allowable for PITI given your current gross monthly income and debts.

DOCUMENT YOUR SPENDING

Category	Current Monthly	Proposed Monthly
Gross Monthly Income	$	$
	$	$
Taxes		
Federal Taxes	$	$
Social Security Taxes	$	$
State and Local Taxes	$	$
Housing Expenses		
Property Taxes	$	$
Home Insurance	$	$
Gas/Electric/Other	$	$
Water/Garbage	$	$
Phone	$	$
TV Cable	$	$
Maintenance	$	$
Repairs	$	$
Food		
Market	$	$
Restaurants/Takeout	$	$
Household		
Clothing/Shoes	$	$
Dry Cleaning	$	$
Haircuts	$	$
Miscellaneous	$	$

DOCUMENT YOUR SPENDING *(cont.)*

Category	*Current Monthly*	*Proposed Monthly*
Consumer Debt		
Auto Loans	$	$
Credit Cards	$	$
Student Loans	$	$
Miscellaneous	$	$
Fun/Entertainment		
Entertainment	$	$
Vacation/Sports	$	$
Gifts	$	$
Pets/Animals	$	$
Health Club/Gym	$	$
Charity	$	$
Healthcare		
Doctors/Hospitals	$	$
Prescriptions	$	$
Dental	$	$
Insurance		
Auto	$	$
Health	$	$
Life/Disability	$	$
Miscellaneous	$	$
Education		
Classes	$	$
Books	$	$
Supplies	$	$

DOCUMENT YOUR SPENDING *(cont.)*

Category	*Current Monthly*	*Proposed Monthly*
Kids		
Day Care	$	$
Sports/Toys	$	$
Child Support	$	$
Other	$	$
Auto/Transportation		
Gasoline	$	$
Maintenance/Repairs	$	$
Other Transportation	$	$
Total Expenses	$	$
Savings Emergency Fund	$	$
Amount Available for Mortgage Payment	$	$

Follow this mathematic formula to calculate:

Gross Income (minus) total expenses (minus) amount saved (equals) the amount available for mortgage payment.

The Home Buying Process

BUYING A HOME is a complicated process, and it can be very intimidating for the first-time buyer. The good news is you've got someone here to help. I'm giving you an easy to follow, step-by-step method that will help you prepare for the ultimate home buying experience.

This starts out approximately six months before you hope to start shopping for a home, but it can be accomplished quicker as long as you walk through all of the steps.

6 MONTHS OUT

Get a copy of your credit report.

Don't leave yourself in a position where you are required to pay off a disputed collection account in order to receive your desired loan. You also don't want to be subject to paying a higher rate of interest unnecessarily because of credit report errors.

Give yourself the necessary time to obtain the optimum credit score so you can qualify for the best rate available when the time comes.

We will be talking later in this book about how to get a free copy of your credit report, how to protect yourself from identity theft, and how to improve your credit score and dispute negative information.

3 MONTHS OUT

Start the interview process.

It is time to start interviewing lenders and individual mortgage professionals. This needs to happen before you even start to sort through your mortgage options. We will be discussing what specific questions you need to ask in a later chapter.

Searching for the perfect loan can be a very overwhelming and stressful experience, especially if you are working with the wrong person or company. Building a good working relationship with your mortgage professional before you go house hunting is vitally important.

It's also extremely important to get pre-approved. This is where some individuals become confused. I'm referring here to credit approval, which is subject to an appraisal. I am not speaking of just pre-qualification. This step needs to be completed prior to doing any serious house shopping. We will be discussing the differences in pre-approval and how to get yourself pre-approved in more detail later.

The other important reason to work with someone you know and trust is because the mortgage industry remains in a constant state of change. Programs are here one day and gone the next. When you are shopping for a lender, I cannot recommend enough that you stay offline.

Shopping for a mortgage online is just a disaster waiting to happen. I don't mean you need to avoid filling out forms online with your local lender—this can be very convenient.

But I do recommend staying away from long-distance online

lenders. You simply will not get the customer service and attention to detail that you need and deserve in this process.

Too many times, I've seen clients not get the loan product or the pricing they were promised. The worst part is they don't discover it until the day of closing. What are you going to do then?

I recommend using a local, experienced mortgage broker in your area for many reasons, but the biggest is that they are not limited to one supply of money, like that of a traditional lender (*such as banks, credit unions, retail mortgage companies*).

They have the ability to provide you with a multitude of options. A mortgage broker will shop different lenders and help you determine which product is the best fit for your needs.

In some cases, they may even be able to negotiate a better deal for you than that of a traditional lender. For a list of licensed mortgage brokers in your area, go to www.NAMB.org and click on the "Find a Broker" link.

When shopping for a mortgage broker, always ask for references. Also ask for their NMLS number and company number. You can use this information to check their status in the Nationwide Mortgage Licensing System at www.nmlsconsumeraccess.org. Simply enter the information they've provided to research their company.

This is a free service to the consumer and allows you to confirm that the mortgage company or individual mortgage professional is authorized to conduct mortgage business in your state.

You can also check with your state authority to see if there are any claims that have been filed against any mortgage professional or company.

I have been a Mortgage Broker for over thirty-seven years, licensed in the state of Oregon from 2001 through 2011. I was always happy to provide my licensing information, testimonials or references at any time. My company license was OR#2416, NMLS company number #266115, and my loan originator NMLS number was #272837. I'm very happy to say that I never had a single claim filed against me in my entire career.

Reduce your credit utilization, don't open or close any accounts.

Make sure that you have the funds needed for down payment and closing costs set aside with a verifiable paper trail in your bank account. Your lender will need to know the source of these funds.

Do you plan on obtaining a gift from a relative? You will need a signed Gift Letter from your Donor and copy of the check from the Donor's account. I have enclosed a sample Gift Letter Form/Certification in the Forms section for your convenience. We will talk more about gifts and down payment requirements in the chapter on loan products.

Do you plan on asking the seller to contribute toward your closing costs? Asking the seller to contribute is always a possibility, so talk to a real estate professional about what's available in the local market.

Begin researching neighborhoods, schools and areas that you like. A licensed Realtor® can help make your house hunt a much easier process.

2 MONTHS OUT

Begin researching interest rates.

Get an idea of what interest rates are today in your area and confirm that the rates have not changed significantly since you became pre-approved.

Make sure that your credit approval is still valid with your mortgage broker. Most pre-approvals are only guaranteed for a specific period of time, typically 90 to120 days.

Double check that none of your financial circumstances have changed since originally talking with your lender. Bring your lender up-to-date on any changes to your financial standing.

THE HOUSE HUNT

Begin comparing available homes in the area.

This is when it gets really exciting! Have your Realtor® begin to show you homes in the areas that you have researched.

Have a "house hunting features" check list handy to jot down all of the items to consider while you are looking at homes.

Some of the basic things to look for are:

- What part of town or neighborhood do you want to live in?
- Do you want an older home or a newer home?
- If schools are a factor, do you want a specific school? Is there bus transportation or are you within walking distance?
- What style of home will you consider: contemporary, traditional, colonial or does it matter? Will you need one story, two story, townhouse/condo or a manufactured home?
- Do you have animals to consider?

Take a lot of notes and maybe snap a picture or two of each house you visit. Write down the likes and dislikes of each one in your notes. It's really difficult to keep everything straight when you have looked at dozens of homes and are trying to sort them out for potential offer possibilities.

And here is a very important tip for you: when you are ready to make an offer on a home, get a "custom fit" copy of your credit approval letter from your lender and submit it with your offer to purchase.

This is one of the questions you will want to ask when interviewing your lender and/or individual mortgage professional, "Do they offer 'custom fit' credit approval letters?"

I always recommend having the letter match your offer exactly. This is to ensure that if you qualify for more than you wish to initially offer, you won't lose any bargaining power by having your credit approval letter show a higher amount. Your mortgage professional should be happy to do this for you. If not, you might think about finding another mortgage broker.

Interviewing Lenders: What to Know, What to Ask

DID YOU KNOW THAT YOU should be the one interviewing your mortgage loan professional, not the other way around?

Earlier, we talked about choosing a lender and shopping for fees. One of the biggest decisions you will make in the Home Buying Process will be choosing and working with a lender. We are not only talking about picking a reliable financial institution, but more importantly a knowledgeable, experienced mortgage professional or loan officer within that financial institution.

Levels of experience can and will vary greatly within a company and you need to work with someone who has adequate experience. Choosing the wrong lender or loan officer could potentially be the biggest headache for anyone in the mortgage process. This one wrong choice can leave behind detrimental ramifications, some of which can last the entire life of your loan.

In other words, it's important to do your homework! The best way to find a reputable, knowledgeable mortgage professional is by personal referral from someone that you know and trust.

I cannot stress enough how important it is to use a reputable independent mortgage broker. They're in the business of shopping and comparing loans, have a variety of different lenders to choose from, will not have a personal interest in one particular mortgage company, and can help you in comparing all the loan costs and features.

There are individuals out there who will tell you that using a mortgage broker will cost you more than using a traditional bank, credit union or retail mortgage lender. But this is simply not true. It depends totally on the individual that you are working with for your loan. So shop around, ask for references, and do your homework.

Here are some of the most important questions to ask when you're initially shopping for a lender/mortgage broker:

- How does their pre-approval process work? Do they offer a formal credit approval or just a pre-qualify process?
- Do they actually provide a credit approval letter? Will they "custom fit" the letter to your offer, even if it needs to be re-issued several times?
- How long does it take to get credit approval, subject to a satisfactory appraisal?
- How long has the mortgage professional or loan officer been in the business? How long has their company been in business? Is the company well known? How long have they worked for their current company?
- Do they have references? What is their NMLS number and their NMLS company number?
- When do they lock-in the interest rate? How long will they guarantee their rate and fees once the loan has been locked? Are there different locking options? If the interest rate goes down before closing on a home, do you get the lower rate?
- Do they provide weekly status updates?
- Does the loan officer or mortgage professional work on commission?

- Is the loan processing handled in the local lending office or off site?

The lender should also offer local processing of the paperwork throughout the loan process. This will ensure that your loan officer is more involved in the day-to-day process and offering a better level of customer service.

It is also vitally important for you to know that a lender cannot accurately quote you an interest rate or loan fees without knowing your credit score and property information.

There are several "add-ons" to loan pricing for items such as credit score, loan purpose, a cash-out refinance, loan to value, property type and others. So when shopping and attempting to compare apples to apples, you must have all this information available for the lender to give you an accurate quote.

Some additional questions you may want to ask each lender you meet with are:

- Does the mortgage broker/loan officer attend their closing appointments?
- How much commission do they want to make on each loan?
- Who pays the Loan Origination Fee?
- How does their interest rate lock policy work? Do they offer Lock Extensions?
- How do they as an individual, keep track of the financial markets?
- Do they actively participate in the locking of the loan, pricing, and what time period it is locked for?

Keeping Score: Understand Your Credit in the Loan Process

THE FIRST STEP in becoming an educated, savvy mortgage shopper is to know your credit rating and credit score. In some cases, people will end up paying a higher interest rate than needed at the last minute. This is simply because they didn't do their homework early to find out exactly what their credit history and credit score looked like.

Let me promise you this: credit report errors do happen!

Order a copy of your credit report about six months before you're ready to start shopping for a home. This ensures that if there are errors, you will have the opportunity to correct any mistakes or dispute items on your report. You want to do this long before you find your dream home and are pressured to close in a 30-day time frame.

I can't tell you the number of times that I've worked with clients who end up paying anywhere from a 0.50 to 1.50% higher interest rate because they didn't have time to fix their credit and satisfy their closing deadline. Over a 30-year period, this can cost you thousands of dollars in unnecessary interest if you're not prepared.

What is a Credit Report?

Your credit report is a history of your credit activities. Items such as:

- Timeliness of payments
- Current debt balances
- Length of credit history
- The amount of credit available to you
- The number of credit inquiries on your behalf
- Any public record or legal action taken against you for non-payment such as bankruptcy, collections, or judgments

The credit scoring systems use your credit history to generate your credit score, sometimes referred to as your FICO score.

Credit scoring is not underwriting a loan, but assessing the risk of repayment based on the consumers payment history and debt utilization. It can also be described as a snapshot of a consumer's credit profile at the particular point in time that a credit report is obtained from the credit reporting agency.

The Federal Credit Reporting Act (FCRA) is enforced by the Federal Trade Commission (FTC) and is aimed at both the Credit Reporting Agencies (CRA) and the creditors supplying the information to the CRA.

The objective is to protect the consumer by ensuring privacy and accuracy of the information being reported. Under the FCRA, a credit reporting agency has five days from the receipt of a written dispute request to contact the appropriate credit grantor about investigating the complaint and receive a reply back within 30 days of the original investigation request.

You can help ensure accuracy by self-monitoring the credit reports from each of the three credit reporting agencies on a regular basis. They work independently and may each be reporting different information. You will not know from which agency your lender will order your credit report, this is why it is advisable to check all three periodically.

As a consumer, you are allowed one free credit report each year. To obtain this report go to www.annualcreditreport.com. This credit report will not include your credit scores. To obtain your credit scores, there will be an additional fee charged.

The Three Credit Reporting Agencies are:

Equifax: www.equifax.com / 800-685-1111

Attention: Consumer Services
P.O. Box 740256
Atlanta, GA 30374

Experian: www.experian.com / 888-397-3742

Attention: Consumer Assistance
P.O. Box 9554
Allen, TX 75013

TransUnion: www.transunion.com / 800-916-8800

Attention: Consumer Assistance
P.O. Box 2000
Chester, PA 19022

When you visit annualcreditreport.com, you will be forwarded to each of the three credit repositories separately to collect your free credit report. In the end, you will have three reports, one from each agency. Print the reports for your information. They contain valuable guidelines on how to read the report and your rights under the Fair Credit Reporting Act.

Two of the agencies will provide your credit score for a small additional fee. TransUnion will invite you to a 7-day free trial of their credit monitoring product in exchange for receiving your credit score. A credit monitoring membership is an annual membership that monitors your credit record and will notify you when someone inquiries about your credit. If you don't want to go through the process of signing up and then cancelling, you're fine with having two out of three credit scores.

Just be sure to check through your TransUnion report, and if nothing derogatory shows up, you should be fine. This is especially true if your other two scores are within close range of each other and at a satisfactory level for loan purposes. A 720 score is your target for optimal pricing.

However, a credit monitoring membership is worth considering if you want to protect your credit. I am a huge advocate of these programs as well as credit fraud protection. It's a great way to stay up-to-date on your credit history. You will also know instantly if there is any evidence of potential identity theft—someone using your personal identifying information without your permission to commit fraud or purchase products and services.

The Federal Trade Commission (FTC) estimates that as many as 9 million Americans have their identities stolen each year. In fact, you or someone you know may have experienced some form of identity theft. (source: http://www.ftc.gov/bcp/edu/microsites/idtheft/)

Identity Theft is serious and can seemingly destroy your life overnight. Identity thieves may rent an apartment, obtain a credit card, or establish a telephone account in your name. You may not find out about the theft until you review your credit report or until you're contacted by a debt collector. This type of crime can be costly, time consuming, and stressful to clean up.

Each of the three credit reporting agencies offers a credit monitoring product, but as with lenders, I think it's important to shop around. The prices for this service will vary greatly from program to program.

How to Dispute Errors on Your Credit Report

Errors on your credit report can have a negative impact on obtaining future credit. Consumers have a right to review their files and dispute any errors or missing information. The credit reporting agency has the obligation to investigate, respond and correct the discrepancies, and notify any recipients within six months of the credit report issue date.

If you discover an error on your credit report, I recommend taking the following steps:

- **Dispute the error in writing.** The consumer must write a letter of dispute regarding a specific piece of information by a specific credit reporting agency referencing the trade line, account numbers and the item being disputed. Send the letter overnight mail, with a return receipt requested, or file it online at the credit reporting agency's website. This date of filing (or receipt by mail) is when the thirty-day investigation timeline begins.

- **Provide very specific information.** Your name, address, social security number for each item of dispute, a request for deletion or correction, and copies of the supporting documentation for the dispute.

- **Keep copies** of your letter of dispute and all supporting documentation.

- **Check all other credit reporting agency reports** to ensure their accuracy. Submit a dispute letter on each specific item to the corresponding creditor if you find it across multiple agency reports.

Within five business days after the completion of a dispute investigation, the credit reporting agency must send a written response to the consumer with its findings along with a copy of the revised report. This letter will indicate:

- There is an error and the credit report is corrected.
- There is no error, so the report will remain as originally submitted.
- The credit grantor did not respond in the allotted time, so the disputed item will be removed from the report.

Ways to Raise Your Credit Score

Credit scores can range from a low of 300 to a high of 850 points. The higher your credit score is, the lower the risk of default is to the potential lender. For home loan purposes, your lender will typically use the middle score of the three scores submitted for loan qualification and pricing purposes.

Raising your credit score is a task that must be accomplished over time. The credit score is an assessment of credit history factors. Therefore, it's extremely difficult to raise your score during the short period of time in which you are applying for a loan.

It's also important to be aware of the positive and negative factors that affect your rating. The higher a key factor or reason code is listed on your report, the more negative weight it's given in the calculation of the FICO score.

- 35% of your score reflects late payments, collections, public records and past due accounts
- 30% is outstanding debt balances on revolving credit

- 15% is length of credit history
- 10% comes from credit inquiries
- 10% other types of credit in use

Here are examples of how different situations will affect your credit score:

- Severity, timeframe and frequency of delinquencies noted on trade lines listed on the credit report within the last 24 months are a primary indicator of risk. Check the date of filing, the more recent the date, the harder the hit will be to your credit score.
- How many trade lines have balances reported close to the high credit balance or credit limit? Higher balances generally indicate greater risk, especially if it's over 50% of the credit line amount.
- Having more than 8 credit cards is considered higher risk. Do not close out accounts unless one of the top key factors or reason codes indicates "too many bank cards." Closing an account that has a zero balance may negatively affect your score.
- Multiple inquiries can potentially take 1–50 points off a consumer's score, depending on the other variables in the report. The average is a 1–35 points lost on inquiry. But be aware that there is no specific value. Try to reduce or eliminate the need for consumer credit inquiries six months prior to obtaining a home loan. It will speed the credit approval process and reduce the need for supportive documentation.

Try to avoid companies that promise to fix your credit for a fee, sometimes referred to as credit repair or rapid re-score companies. The best way to clean up your credit is to do the work yourself and establish positive credit habits. An example of positive credit habits include:

- Make payments on time
- Pay down credit cards
- Charge small amounts and pay them off in full each month
- Monitor all three credit reporting agencies on an annual basis
- Research alternative lending sources, which can help you re-establish credit and recover from damaged credit history though they may charge higher rates
- Create a savings account for emergencies and a down payment to help the lender feel at ease
- Explain one-time digressions as lenders will take these one-time occurrences under consideration
- Read what you sign and beware of blank or fill-in-later documents

There are a number of services out there that claim to clean up or "fix" your credit, whether the items are correct or not. They are using the Fair Credit Reporting Act (FCRA) to often manipulate the 30-day investigation process.

Sometimes it works, sometimes it doesn't. But they will always charge you a fee for their services. This fee can be very expensive and comes with no guarantees. And if they try to dispute a correct item on your credit report, it could be construed as fraud.

No one knows your credit or your history better than you. Take some time to get informed, and then take the necessary steps to ensure your credit score is as high as it can be before you apply for a home loan.

It's Time to Secure Your Loan

THE HOME LOAN PROCESS is defined by what takes place during and after you have an accepted sales agreement. Let's discuss a step-by-step view of what happens during the loan process—from credit approval to closing and moving into your new home—to establish what you can expect along the way. There are many assorted forms and paperwork necessary to purchase a home, and a number of important steps in the process.

Step 1

As a prospective buyer, once you have selected your mortgage professional to work with, it's time to get pre-approved. We are going to discuss this step in further detail during the following chapter, but know that it is the first and most vital step towards your closing day.

Step 2

You've received pre-approval and have your maximum loan amount available. You understand the down payment that is required for the program you've selected. You know what your maximum sales price range is, and now you are ready to go house hunting.

At this point, you've done your neighborhood research and have an idea what type of property you like best. After viewing many homes, you find a home that meets all or most of your requirements and you make an offer. Your Realtor® will need a custom fit pre-approval letter from your mortgage professional to submit with your offer. They can help make the negotiation process so much smoother and stress free.

Step 3

Your offer is accepted and you receive an accepted purchase agreement. A purchase agreement is usually more than 10 pages long and can contain several necessary addendums. These addendums are designed to help protect you, so it's nice to know you have a professional Realtor® looking out for your best interest. We will be discussing the advantages of using one later in this book.

Step 4

The accepted purchase agreement is then delivered to your lender and that's when it gets really exciting! You have just made a formal loan application. Now the clock starts running and everyone scurries to meet your specified closing date.

Step 5

It's now time to *lock-in* your interest rate or make the decision to *float* the rate until a later date prior to your closing. For ensuring you get a great rate, I am going to share with you all the insider tips I've learned in thirty-seven years in an upcoming chapter.

Step 6

The lender orders the title work and appraisal. If these come back acceptable, you then move on to Step 7.

If there are any issues with the appraisal (*for example the value comes back less than sales price*) the realtors, seller and buyer are all notified. There are several options to help get the issue resolved and your Realtor® will help you navigate those options. Any missing or additional supportive documentation that is needed will be requested at this time.

Step 7

Your file is then sent to underwriting for final approval. Once the appraisal is settled, the designated underwriter for your lender will review the file and re-submit it into their automated underwriting system (AUS) for final approval or what's sometimes referred to as a firm commitment.

If your mortgage professional has done their job well, there will very rarely be any surprises at this point in the process. I can tell you from years of experience that most delays at final underwriting are due to a lack of communication between your loan officer and the underwriter.

The other issue may be that your loan officer did not submit a complete file. They have a checklist of items that the underwriter originally asked for and it is just a matter of getting the supportive documentation that was requested. At this point, you receive final approval and the loan file is ready to go to the closing department for loan documents to be drawn.

Step 8

You provide the lender with the homeowner's insurance binder that you received from your agent. Your insurance agent will need the mortgagee clause—a clause that indicates the payee information in case of loss as required by your lender—to complete the binder. Your mortgage professional will provide you with this information.

Step 9

Closing documents are prepared and sent to the Escrow Company or attorney for closing. Appointments are scheduled for signing. Your Realtor® and mortgage professional should attend the closing appointment. Make sure you ask your mortgage professional if they attend their closings during the interview process. This is very important and can help eliminate clerical errors that might otherwise get missed at closing.

Step 10

It's Closing Day! You are finally ready to move to your new home. Your loan was approved, your home has passed all inspections, you're packed and you can't wait to get the keys to your new home.

But before that can happen, you must go to closing. A closing is a meeting where all individuals involved with the transaction sign the final closing statement, loan documents and deeds required to transfer the title of the property to you. We will go over what those documents usually consist of, in more detail during a later chapter.

Pre-Approval and What It Means for You

MORTGAGE REGULATIONS have experienced consistent change over the last few years due to the credit crisis. Whether you are about to buy your first home, are refinancing or planning a move to your next home, it is critical that you inform yourself with the new credit requirements.

Programs and lender requirements change on a daily basis, so getting pre-approved before you go house shopping can save you time, money and stress. They are easy and provide peace of mind when shopping for your home.

Your lender or mortgage broker can provide you with a written pre-approval letter at little to no cost. And yes, there is a difference between getting pre-qualified and actually getting pre-approved!

A pre-approval or credit approval is obtained when the lender or mortgage broker pulls a credit report and actually submits your credit profile to a lender.

A credit approval letter is as good as money in the bank and can help with your negotiation process when bidding on a specific home. A seller will always look more favorably at an offer that is "credit approved" than an offer that is not.

You will also want to ask your mortgage professional to custom fit your credit approval letter when it is presented to the seller so that it matches the offer you wish to make. This will help your negotiating power without giving away the fact that you may qualify for an amount larger than you wish to offer.

The pre-approval process begins by submitting a completed mortgage loan application, known as an Uniform Residential Loan Application or FNMA 1003 Form.

This mortgage loan application includes several sections that will collect information about you, your overall finances, loan type and property details. It consists of several pages and at first glance, can be a little intimidating or complicated. When broken down a section at a time, it can be easily and accurately completed. If you do have questions in any particular area, save the application and your mortgage professional will be able to help you.

All of your personal information on your application is confidential and protected by law. If you put false or inaccurate information on the application, it can have a serious impact on your chances of being approved and could be illegal.

Attempt to complete as much of the application as you can instead of relying on someone else to complete it for you. It's a much safer solution when it comes to protecting yourself from fraud or having any of your information altered.

Remember that in order to protect yourself and your credit, you never want to sign any blank or incomplete forms. Don't let someone convince you that your mortgage professional or others involved will fill it in later.

This is a disaster waiting to happen and YOU are ultimately responsible for anything that you sign. Never sign any document that you do not understand, and don't allow anyone to pressure you into signing any document or contract that you don't want to sign.

There are a total of 10 sections on the Uniform Residential Loan Application that will be described in detail on the following pages. Your mortgage professional can help you with the specific product type, term and interest rate on the day of application. If you are a little unsure, please don't stress and just complete the items that you can for now.

At this point, you should have a good idea of the loan amount that you wish to apply for. If not, go back and complete the monthly spending analysis. At the very least, you should have a rough estimate of the maximum monthly payment you wish to consider.

In the following pages, I have broken down each of the ten application sections with instructions as to what information you will need for each.

Section I: Type of Mortgage and Terms of Loan

The information in this section should match the type of mortgage and terms that you have discussed with your mortgage professional. For a purchase transaction where you have not selected a property, you can specify the "maximum" amount that you wish to borrow.

Section II: Property Information and Purpose of Loan

If you are completing the loan application for pre-approval purposes on a purchase transaction, you may list "address to be determined" in the subject property field.

If you have selected a home or if this loan is for a refinance, you will need to provide information about the property including the address, year built, and whether you want to purchase or refinance.

If the loan is for a refinance or for proposed construction, the other property information will need to be completed.

Section III: Borrower Information

This is where you list your personal information including that of a co-borrower—an additional person who accepts responsibility for paying back your home loan such as your husband or wife. You will need to provide your social security number, marital status, dependents and contact information here.

If you have lived at your current address for less than two years, you will need to provide additional residential addresses to cover a minimum two-year period.

Your lender will use this information to order your credit report, so make sure this information is accurate!

Section IV: Employment Information

You will need to provide a history of your employment for the last two-year period. If you work multiple jobs, you will also need to include a two-year history of working multiple jobs for that information to be considered in your income analysis. You will need to include an accurate mailing address and contact information for all of your employers.

Your lender may send a Verification of Employment (VOE) form to the employers you have listed to verify salary, overtime or commission pay. Having accurate information listed on the application will prevent any delays in receiving this information in a timely manner.

Section V: Monthly Income and Combined Housing Expense Information

Use your gross income (before taxes or deductions) for the monthly income column. This will include most sources of income itemized as indicated on the form. You are not required to disclose alimony, child support, or separate maintenance payments if you do not choose to have them considered as income for paying your home loan.

You will also need to provide the last thirty days of payroll stubs with year-to-date earnings, and your last two years W-2 forms and federal tax returns, including all schedules for verification. Again, be as accurate as possible to avoid delays.

Section VI: Assets and Liabilities

Section VI reflects your current financial position including what you own (*assets*) and how much you owe (*liabilities*). The lender will subtract the value of your liabilities from your assets to determine your net worth.

Bank accounts, savings, retirement funds, investments, life insurance, vehicles, furnishings and other personal property can be used as assets to support your application. You will also need to provide your bank account statements for the last two months as supportive documentation. Other assets will not usually need to be verified unless they will be liquidated for use as part of your down payment.

Liabilities will include items such as car loans, credit cards, finance company loans, bank and credit union loans or any other existing mortgages, including Home Equity Loans.

Section VII: Details of the Transaction

This section gives the itemized details of the home purchase transaction. Your loan officer or mortgage professional will complete this area of the application.

Section VIII: Declarations

In this section, you will be asked to answer questions about any pending legal issues or other factors that may affect your financial situation both past and present.

For example, "*Have you filed bankruptcy in the last 7 years?*" This information, along with your credit report and any written explanation you may provide, will help your lender's underwriter to assess your ability to pay the mortgage.

You will also be asked to confirm your intent to occupy the property and also affirm if you are a U.S. citizen or permanent resident alien.

Section IX: Acknowledgment and Agreement

In this section, you sign your name indicating the information you have provided is accurate and true to the best of your knowledge. Remember, your signature is your word of honor.

Section X: Information for Government Monitoring Purposes

This section requests you to provide information as to your race and ethnic origin. This information is documented because the U.S. government wants to be sure our housing finance system meets the needs of every racial and ethnic group in our country. This is one way to gather the statistics necessary to track this information.

After the lender and underwriter review your loan application, along with a copy of your credit report, they will make the decision to issue a credit approval letter subject to a satisfactory property.

Congratulations! You are now pre-approved. Grab your letter and get ready to go house hunting.

Finding the Right Loan for You

DO YOU KNOW HOW TO PROTECT YOURSELF from predatory lending? Education is the key.

In the past, predatory lending was a huge problem. Many potential homeowners were taken advantage of because they had a bad financial situation or less than perfect credit.

With liberal underwriting, low rates, a multitude of programs, and a booming housing market, it was often standard practice to charge higher interest rates and fees or both, as well as less attractive mortgage terms. Teaser rates and adjustable rate mortgages (ARMS) with negative amortization—also known as "pick-a-payment plan" mortgages—were flooding the market place.

A loan with negative amortization is a loan where the minimum required monthly payment does not pay the entire monthly interest due or any principle balance. The balance continues to grow instead of being reduced with regular scheduled monthly payments.

No documentation loans (no doc) and reduced documentation loans (reduced doc) were also popular, each covering a different segment of the borrowing market. These types of products were designed for individuals that were qualified borrowers, but had complex financial statements that were difficult or time consuming to document. However, they were not always used for their intended purpose. Every lender had their own version of these products, paying mortgage brokers and in-house loan officers big bucks to sell them.

The justification for this type of price gouging was that a loan of this type was considered to be high risk, but because the lenders and their investors wanted everyone to experience home ownership, they were glad to help out. Even though it's true these types of loans posed greater potential for default, it was also true that individuals with credit issues have fewer options available to them. Instead of taking the time to get credit problems corrected before buying, it was easier to just put a financial Band-Aid on it with the promise of fixing it later.

I don't want you to think I am putting all the blame on lenders or the individuals that sold these products. I believe it's also the consumer's responsibility to know what they're getting into prior to signing on the dotted line. It seemed to me like consumers were relying on others to make their financial decisions for them and that's when things began to get scary.

Even more unbelievable to me, people were racing into the housing market and jumping on the band-wagon through bidding wars on homes, often paying more than the home was appraised for believing they would make up the difference down the road. With things changing quickly as prices climbed, it proved too difficult to keep up.

People were not making sound, unemotional business decisions. Instead, they were doing anything they could to get their piece of the American housing pie.

Due to the collapse of the housing market, the mortgage credit crisis, and the tightening of mortgage underwriting requirements, this type of high risk financing has now pretty much disappeared and as a result, we are all paying for it.

Today, loans fall into three basic categories:

- Conventional, conforming loans: loans sold to Fannie Mae (FNMA) and Freddie Mac (FHLMC)
- Government loans: FHA, VA and USDA Rural Housing
- Non-conforming or "hard money" loans

In addition, each one of these categories will offer their own version of fixed rate products and adjustable rate products, both conforming and non-conforming.

We will not explore each of these particular products in depth, but we will be discussing the features of these products in general terms. This will help you understand which features, either fixed rate or adjustable rate, are best suited for your individual circumstances.

Please, don't let the term "adjustable rate mortgage" scare you. There are some very good adjustable rate loans out there that will save you thousands of dollars in interest, if you know what to look for and how to protect yourself. You need to evaluate the risk of an adjustable rate mortgage (ARM) with how long you plan on living in the home and whether or not you will keep the home when you move.

In addition to those factors, take into consideration whether or not your income will fluctuate in the future. Is it likely to grow or are you on a salary that is pretty much fixed? Adjustable rate mortgages are loans with pre-determined periodic adjustments and are marvelous financial tools if used correctly. But they do not fit well with every borrower. That is a decision only YOU can make.

Conventional conforming loans are sold to Fannie Mae and Freddie Mac. They offer some exceptional fixed period adjustable rate mortgage (ARM) loans with varying terms—loans that provide fixed-rate terms for five years, seven years, or even ten years before they begin any adjustments.

These types of loans will usually offer a lower interest rate than a thirty-year fixed-rate term, and can potentially save a savvy borrower thousands of dollars in yearly interest.

I do not recommend the use of short term ARMs such as one-year or three-year fixed period. This is due to the fact that big adjustments to your rate and monthly payments can happen quickly and it's proven difficult for the average consumer to budget for those types of quick changes.

Adjustable rate mortgages (ARMs) are not for individuals who are:

- On a fixed income or a one-income family
- A first-time home buyer
- Attempting to qualify for a larger loan amount by utilizing a lower initial interest rate

They are perfect loans for borrowers who will stay in a home for a short period of time. If you plan on staying in your home for five years, pick a product such as the seven-year fixed period ARM to give yourself a little breathing room just in case things don't go as you have planned.

You will save a lot of money in interest over that of a thirty-year fixed-rate product and still have the security of a fixed rate for that short term period of time. Fixed-period ARMs will also have different rate indexes, margins, adjustment caps, and lifetime adjustment caps. So it pays you in the end to find out how the particular ARM you are considering will adjust and under what terms.

A "rate index" is best described as a regularly published rate—independent of the lending institution—that measures the prevailing cost of funds. It is used periodically with the margin to set adjustable rate mortgage accrual rates or the stated annual rate at which interest is calculated. Among the most common are the one-year, Constant-Maturity Treasury (CMT) securities, the Cost of Funds Index (COFI), and the London Interbank Offered Rate (LIBOR).

The lender sometimes refers to the "margin" as "the spread." It is the amount the lender adds to the index to determine the fully indexed accrual rate. Another way to look at it is that the margin usually reflects the profit the lender will receive above the cost of funds as a whole.

An "adjustment cap" is a limitation on how much an interest rate on an adjustable rate mortgage can change—up or down—during a predetermined adjustment period. An adjustment period can be one, three, five, seven or ten years depending on the individual loan product chosen.

A "life-time adjustment cap" is a limitation on how much an interest rate can move up or down on an adjustable rate mortgage during the life-time payment schedule of the loan chosen.

Loans with fixed rate terms—a rate that remains the same throughout the entire payment schedule of the loan—will usually be the best conservative approach for first-time home buyers, one-income households, or individuals on a fixed income. The fixed rate products will offer different terms, with fifteen, twenty, and thirty-year terms being the most popular.

How to Evaluate and Compare Mortgage Products

When evaluating products, it is important to base your decision on how long you expect to live in the home as opposed to items such as the closing costs, out of pocket cash requirements, or the total cost of interest over the life of the loan.

For example, let's say that you are looking at a $125,000 purchase price with 20% down payment—a $100,000 loan—and you plan on living in the home for approximately five years. In this particular example, we will assume that the other closing costs for all three types of loans are the same at $3,775.00.

In our scenario, you have 3 options available to you:

- Conventional thirty-year fixed rate loan at 6.00% with a 1% loan origination fee
- Conventional seven-year fixed period ARM (7/1) at 4.75% with a 1% loan origination fee and thirty-year amortization
- Conventional thirty-year fixed rate loan at 5.50% with a 2% loan origination fee

Now let's look at each loan individually to compare.

Loan #1: Conventional thirty-year fixed rate loan

- Interest rate: 6.00%
- Origin fee: $1,000
- Closing costs: $3,775
- Total loan (including private mortgage insurance): $100,000
- Monthly payment (principle and interest): $599.55
- Total Payments over five years: $35,973

Loan #2: Conventional seven-year fixed period ARM (7/1)

- Interest rate: 4.75%
- Origin fee: $1,000

- Closing costs: $3,775
- Total loan (including private mortgage insurance): $100,000
- Monthly payment (principle and interest): $521.64
- Total Payments over five years: $31,298.40

Loan #3: Conventional thirty-year fixed rate loan

- Interest rate: 5.50%
- Origin fee: $2,000
- Closing costs: $3,775
- Total loan (including private mortgage insurance): $100,000
- Monthly payment (principle and interest): $567.79
- Total Payments over five years: $34,067.40

If you look at your total out of pocket cash requirement (*your monthly payments plus the origin fee and closing costs*) for each loan, you'll see the adjustable rate mortgage provides a significant savings.

- Loan #1: $40,748.00
- Loan #2: $36,073.40
- Loan #3: $39,842.40

In this example, the seven-year fixed period ARM is the best choice for our borrower and actually saves $4,674.60 in total out of pocket cash.

You can also see that the thirty-year fixed rate at 5.50% with a 2% fee was not necessarily a better deal than the thirty-year fixed rate at 6.00% with 1% fee. In this example, the borrower would have saved only

$905.60 over their five-year ownership period. This example illustrates how important it is to evaluate your options to determine the break-even point.

Evaluating an adjustable rate mortgage over the life of the loan can be difficult. Some experts suggest you evaluate it as a worst case example with the maximum interest rate adjustments.

The truth is that the chances of the loan going to the maximum interest rate at each adjustment period is not likely and in most cases, evaluating it in this manner will not give you accurate information. So evaluate the loan only over the period of time that you plan on living in the home or will likely be making some changes to your financing.

Buying down the interest rate and paying a higher loan origination fee can also be a very cost effective option, but only if you are going to stay in the home for an extended period of time.

Another factor in determining your perfect loan product is the down payment requirements. These will vary from program to program, and there is a delicate balance when determining which option is right for you.

A down payment of 20% or more of the purchase price on a conventional loan product will typically get you a better deal in terms of interest rate and can save you thousands of dollars interest over the life of the loan.

However, pulling too much money out of your own pocket can also be a problem if you need cash later and have invested all of your funds in your home. It can often be difficult to get that money back in case of emergency.

Keep in mind that the amount of money you put down needs to be balanced against your future needs for cash and other purposes such as investments, retirement programs, college and unexpected expenses. We will be discussing these emergency savings options in more detail later.

On conventional conforming loans, you will usually have the option of putting five, ten, fifteen, twenty or more percent down at closing. Each one of these options carries with it a different set of requirements as far as rate, fees and the requirement for private mortgage insurance.

Private mortgage insurance (PMI) is an insurance that offers protection to the lender against the borrower's default on a mortgage loan. If you pay less than 20% down payment, mortgage insurance is going to be required on your loan.

The cost of private mortgage insurance will vary based on the amount of your down payment. This is due to the fact that a 95% loan-to-value ratio is a much higher risk than a 90% or 85% loan. There are also different options or payment plans depending on the specific program requirements.

Some plans offer up-front or all-in-one premiums, while others allow you to "finance" the mortgage insurance premiums over the life of the loan. You can also choose to pay monthly. We will be talking about how to evaluate these private mortgage insurance options, their costs and overall effect on your home loan later in this book.

However much you choose to spend, the entire down payment is usually required to come from the borrower's own funds. There are some programs that will allow a portion of the down payment to come from cash gifts from relatives.

A signed gift letter or certification is required to be signed by both the borrower(s) and the donor(s) providing the gift. These funds must be verified as a gift with no repayment expected or implied. Evidence in the form of bank statements and a copy of the certified check, personal check, or electronic transfer will be required to demonstrate the ability of the donor to give the gift.

The funds given to the applicant cannot be made available to the donor from any person or entity with an interest in the transaction or the subject property. This includes the seller, real estate agents, broker, builder, loan officer or any other entity associated with them.

And buyers should note that it is a Federal crime, punishable by fine, imprisonment or both, to knowingly make any false statements when applying for a mortgage, as applicable under the provision of Title 18, United States Code, Section 1014 and Section 1010.

In other words, be honest and forthcoming about the source of funding for your down payment and have documented evidence of its origination.

Other acceptable sources of down payment include:

- The sale or liquidation of an documentable asset
- A short term loan or liquidation of a retirement account
- A secured equity loan or line of credit from other residential property
- Funds held in a checking, savings, or investment account belonging to the borrower(s)
- Any secured loan, such as refinance of a paid automobile, as long as the new payment is included in the total debt ratio

The lender will require you to provide evidence of any source of funds used as down payment. For example, if you sell an automobile, acceptable documentation would include a copy of the following:

- Vehicle title showing transfer to the purchaser
- Bill of sale
- Certified check or electronic transfer of funds
- Evidence that the funds have been deposited into the borrower's account

Sources of down payment that usually are not allowed:

- Credit card advances or unsecured loans
- Cash on hand with no evidence of source
- Contributions from the seller or other interested parties in the transaction

It is important to understand that these guidelines are the general rule, but will vary by program. Some first-time home buyer programs or government sponsored specialty loans may have different requirements. Always ask your mortgage professional about specific guidelines for the program that you're interested in.

Government loans such as FHA, Federal VA, and USDA Rural Housing products also serve a valuable segment of the borrowing market, but it is important to realize there are trade-offs. These types of loans will usually be less credit score driven, often have more lenient underwriting guidelines, and Federal VA and USDA Rural Housing offer zero down, 100% loan options.

These loans will have extremely high private mortgage insurance premiums or funding fee requirements. This can make your overall loan balance several thousand dollars higher depending on the loan amount as well as any monthly mortgage insurance requirements.

Make sure when evaluating the different products available to you that these mortgage insurance and funding fee costs are included in your overall evaluation.

Non-conforming or "hard money" loans are a specialty type of loan product based solely on the overall asset value of the property. These types of loans are used as a short term financial Band-Aid and are not for the typical homeowner. So be aware if this type of loan is recommended.

Hard money loans are usually issued by private investors. Interest rates are typically higher than conventional residential property loans because of the risk and will have shorter loan periods associated with them. Most hard money loans are used for projects lasting from a few months to a few years.

Hard money is similar to a bridge loan which means it bridges a gap between need and a conforming housing loan. This type of loan will have underwriting criteria and documentation requirements, as well as costs to the borrower.

The primary difference is that a bridge loan often refers to a commercial property or an investment property that may be in transition and does not yet qualify for traditional financing.

A "hard money" loan often refers to not only an asset-based loan with a high interest rate. It can also possibly refer to a distressed financial situation such as an overdue balance on the existing mortgage, or a situation where bankruptcy and foreclosure proceedings are occurring.

The qualifying criteria for a "hard money" loan vary widely by lender and loan purpose. Credit scores, income and other conventional lending criteria will also be analyzed.

Most hard money lenders primarily qualify a loan amount based on the value of the real estate being used as collateral. Typically, the biggest loan one can expect would be about 65% of the property value. That is, if the property is worth $100,000, the lender would advance $65,000 against it. This low loan to value provides added security for the lender, in case of default.

Lock-In Your Lowest Possible Interest Rate

ONE OF THE MOST IMPORTANT ASPECTS of obtaining a mortgage is getting the best interest rate. But it can also be the most difficult. Many borrowers rely on their bank or mortgage broker to secure their interest rate. They give this high level of trust without researching rates or understanding how they change on their own.

Whether you are someone interested in the financial markets or not, it's wise to gain a better understanding of how interest rates are determined, how they move and most importantly, why they change.

Residential mortgage interest rates, and their daily fluctuation in pricing, are determined from the performance of long-term mortgages sold on the secondary market (Wall Street) and packaged into mortgage-backed securities (MBS or mortgage bonds). They are not influenced by U.S. ten-year treasury notes, which is a common misconception.

Following the FNMA thirty-year mortgage bond, along with the 25-day moving average, will always be a good indicator of what rates are doing.

Then you can start to add-in other factors such as:

- Job reports

- The Consumer Price Index
- Gross Domestic Product
- Home sales
- The Consumer Confidence Index
- "Fed Minutes" or changes to the Federal Funds Rate

It can all add up to an incredibly exciting and challenging change to forecast. But don't let that overwhelm you. I can help you better understand interest rate changes and show you what questions to ask.

This does make it all the more important to work with a mortgage professional that is on top of what's going on in the market at any given moment and not someone just looking at a rate sheet. You need someone one your side who understands the deeper causes at work within the market.

In addition to the general list of questions you want to ask when interviewing lenders (*see earlier chapter*), I would encourage you to ask and take diligent notes on the following specific points to ensure your best possible interest rate.

- **Does the lender work on commission?**
- **How much commission do they want to receive on each loan?** Hold out for the straight answer as some mortgage professionals may be shocked by this question. The standard rate falls between 1-1.5% fee on each loan they originate.
- **Who pays that loan origination fee?** If you are not paying it, the lender is pricing the loan higher so they can pay the fee. This is not a great deal for you, especially if you plan to live in the home a

long period of time. You will be paying interest on that fee for the entire life of your loan.

- **Do the interest rates they offer change more than once a day?** Find out how your mortgage professional keeps track of what the financial markets are doing and their effect on interest rates. Ask specific questions about how they monitor and adjust rates based on the market. Find out if they have the ability to anticipate rate changes and when they will notify you rates are about to change.
- **What is their interest rate lock policy?** Ask if the interest rate is automatically locked-in at application. You need to know if you are going to have the ability to play the market and take advantage of any decreases that may come up during the loan process. You also want to gauge their ability to help you in doing just that. Also find out if they offer shorter term locks on rates of less than thirty to forty-five days.

Remember . . . this is one of the biggest purchases you will make in your life time! Make sure that you are working with someone that you feel comfortable with and trust to get you the best rate possible. Build that relationship before you even begin the house hunting process and this entire process will go a lot smoother, plus save you thousands.

Don't wait until you're in the middle of a thirty-day closing and get stuck with whatever is given to you. I hate to say it, but there are times when lenders will quote you one rate, and once they get you in the door things change. It is vitally important to research and choose wisely during this process.

There are new disclosure laws indicating that once you sign a good faith estimate, the terms of the loan cannot change. This is still not always totally true in every case. You will have the opportunity to "lock-in" the interest rate at application or allow the interest rate to float until a later time during the application process.

This "lock-in" time period, in which the lender guarantees an interest rate, is typically specified by a number of days. Typical terms will be ten, thirty, forty-five or sixty-day periods. Pricing will usually be better with shorter lock periods because there is less risk or exposure to the changing market for the lender.

It's important to note that locking in the interest rate at the start of the application is not always the best option for the borrower. This is why the relationship with their mortgage broker becomes extremely important.

As a mortgage broker, I followed the financial markets hourly. I loved playing market and took great pride in getting my borrowers the best deal.

I built a relationship with them in the beginning, explaining that my fee was a fixed fee (*usually 1.00% of the loan amount*) and that it did not change regardless of the pricing that I obtained for them in the market.

I was so aware of the financial markets on any given day, I could watch pricing for them and "lock-in" an interest rate when the market was at its best. That's why it's so important to use a mortgage broker, because they can shop many lenders looking for aggressive pricing. When you work with a bank, you get what they've got with no other options.

There were many times over the course of my career that I caught pricing just right and literally saved my clients hundreds of dollars in origination fees by catching a down trend in the market. I loved being the bearer of good news and my clients felt comfortable knowing that I didn't adjust their rate to obtain a higher fee.

Some lenders will offer a daily interest rate, rarely having mid-day price changes. This is not realistic of what's actually going on in the market. It may seem better from outside appearances, but actually they are hedging the market to offer a slightly higher interest rate. Essentially, they are absorbing any daily market fluctuations and passing it on to the consumer.

It's also important to beware of anyone offering an interest rate considerably less than everyone else you have talked to. I can almost guarantee you that it's probably a bait and switch situation, unless they can reasonably explain why the rate is different.

- Is there a "prepayment penalty?"
- Is there a "temporary buy down" in the rate?

Often a lender will offer better pricing with a prepayment penalty for early payoff. Some of these penalties can be huge, so be careful and always ask for all the details of any fee or penalty term.

A "temporary buy down" is just exactly what it sounds like—a pre-determined, temporary buy down of the interest rate for the first few years of the loan term. There are usually varying options such a 3–2–1 buy down or a 2–1 buy down.

On the 3-2-1 buy down, the interest rate is reduced 3% the first year, 2% the second year, and 1% the third year, years 4-30 are then calculated at the standard 30-year fixed rate.

For example, if you had a thirty-year fixed rate at 7%, the borrower would receive 4% the first year, 5% the second year, 6% for the third year, and then the remaining twenty-seven years would be at a rate of 7%.

With interest rates at record lows, a temporary buy down doesn't seem to be as critical now as it was in years past. However, can you imagine using a 2-1 buy down today? Your first year rate would be at 2%, second year rate at 3%, and remaining years at 4%, an unbelievable interest rate.

However, the "temporary buy down" has a required up-front fee, which usually consists of a calculation of the interest due during that first three-year period at the actual market rate.

This can be a little expensive if paid by the borrower, but can be a wonderful bargaining tool if you ask the seller to pay it. Instead of offering a lower price on the house, ask the seller to pay for a "temporary buy down."

For the first-time home buyer, this can be an excellent resource and help you ease into the routine of making regular house payments. If you are considering a buy down, ask your real estate professional or mortgage broker to you help you structure it.

Also, asking the seller to help pay some of your closing costs can help you get a better interest rate by using the seller's funds to buy down the market rate or pay "discount points." There are rules on how much the seller is allowed to contribute and these vary by program. Just ask your mortgage professional to be sure of what is allowed within your particular loan program.

Here is an example of what a 3-2-1 temporary buy down and a 2-1 buy down would look like. This example is based on a $100,000 loan, 30-year fixed rate mortgage at 7%.

Year (*Interest Rate*): Full Payment | 3-2-1 Payment | 2-1 Payment

Year 1 (4.00%): $665.31 | $477.42 | $536.83

Year 2 (5.00%): $665.31 | $536.83 | $599.56

Year 3 (6.00%): $665.31 | $599.56 | $665.31

Years 4 to 30 (7.00%): $665.31 | $665.31 | $665.31

Cost to fund the buy down: (3-2-1) $4,586.00 | (2-1) $2,331.00

The Truth about Pricing

It's no longer possible to call a lender and ask for an accurate interest rate up-front. Each of the individual loan products have various interest rates, as well as "add-ons" to pricing for different loan characteristics. A lender will need to know all aspects of the transaction to even begin to quote an accurate rate and fee. This is even more difficult when coupled with the fact that interest rates can potentially change several times a day.

Here are some loan factors that are considered "add-ons" to pricing and can affect your interest rate:

- High loan to value
- Credit score (add-ons for credit score can be huge, as much as 1–1.50% in rate, depending on the score)
- Property type (for example a 3-4 unit property, 2 unit property, condo, manufactured housing)
- Subordinate financing (situations where a combined second mortgage is allowed)
- Property use or purpose (second home or investment property)
- If the loan is a "cash out" refinance (the homeowner draws on their equity and pulls out cash for other purposes)
- "Lock-in" periods (time in which a particular interest rate and loan origination fee is guaranteed)
- "Lock-in" extensions (a one-time extension of a particular "lock-in" period for an additional fee)

- Property tax and insurance reserve waiver (escrow waiver)

A reserve or escrow account is an account established for the borrower where one-twelfth of the annual property taxes and hazard insurance are collected monthly with the mortgage payment (PITI). They are reserved here for payment of those items when due. On loan to values below 80%, the borrower can elect to pay their own taxes and insurance when due.

That was a lot to cover, but NOW you're prepared and understand the different variables that can affect your loan!

How to Negotiate Closing Costs

CLOSING COSTS ARE STANDARD COSTS of every loan. There are other fees that can be added in to the cost of a loan solely to increase the lender's profits. These types of costs are usually referred to as junk fees.

These types of fees can be avoided and not all mortgage brokers or lenders charge them.

Examples of items that may be considered junk fees include:

- Processing fee between $250 to $350
- Administration fee on average between $100 to $300
- Wire fees estimated around $100
- Courier fees estimated around $100
- Document preparation fees between $150 to $250

You can see that with just these fees alone, a lender could obtain up to $1100 in extra profits on every single loan they originate.

For comparison, standard or normal closing costs will include:

- Title insurance with costs varying by loan amount, type, and specific coverage required

- Escrow or attorney fees with costs varying by the sale price
- Appraisal fee ranging from $295 to $500 depending on type required and property location (requested by lender and borrower has no input)
- Credit report fee ranging from $12 to $30 depending on the reporting agency selected
- Tax service fee averaging around $60
- Flood determination fee averaging around $17
- Recording fees which vary by county
- Private mortgage insurance which vary by program type and loan amount

This is not an all-inclusive list of standard closing costs. The fees depend on which state you live in, but they should not deviate much, if at all, between various lenders.

Most wholesale lenders will charge mortgage brokers an underwriting fee that is then passed on to the consumer, but that does not necessarily mean working with a mortgage broker will cost you more.

In most cases, this fee will be offset by other less expensive closing costs or origination fees. Mortgage lenders make money based on the size of your loan amount, the discount points, and the loan origination fees you pay.

Discount points are a one-time charge by the lender to buy down a potential interest rate to a rate that is considered below market. This is sometimes referred to in the industry as a "par" rate.

The fee will vary depending on the level of discounted rate. It's usually not cost effective to pay more than 1% in additional discounts to buy the loan down to a below market rate, unless you plan on living in the home a long period of time. You just end up in a pay-me-now instead of later situation.

A loan origination fee is the standard fee that a lender will charge a borrower for obtaining a mortgage. This fee can vary and is based on whether or not the loan is at market rate. The loan can be priced higher to reduce the fee. In my experience, the standard fee is usually about 1%.

We have talked about loan origination fees and discount points in the previous chapter, but it is important to realize that all of these fees may be paid in a variety ways to "custom fit" each borrower's situation. A portion of them can sometimes be financed, paid by the seller, or even reduced by pricing the loan slightly higher resulting in the lender paying the cost.

The option that works best for you can only be determined by getting a "good faith estimate" from your mortgage professional on all of the loan products that you are considering and then using the loan evaluation worksheet in the *Conquer Your Closing Workbook* to compare them.

A good faith estimate (GFE) should provide you with an accurate estimate of your mortgage loan terms and closing costs, also known as settlement charges. Your lender is required by Federal law to provide you with a good faith estimate within three business days of completing a credit application.

The good faith estimate is a three-page form with summary information of the loan terms on the first page, details of your costs or settlement charges on the second page, and optional comparison tables on the third page. These tables allow you to compare rates and fees from other lenders.

The new good faith estimate form, which was designed to improve disclosure clarity, is difficult to understand and not always accurately completed. Completing your own loan evaluation worksheet from the *Conquer Your Closing Workbook* will give a much clearer picture. Compare each individual cost in an itemized manner to ensure you are comparing apples to apples.

It's also important to note that just because you get approved with one lender; it doesn't mean you can't switch lenders prior to finding a property should the situation warrant it. Where it becomes difficult to switch is after an appraisal is completed, so it pays to do as much homework upfront as possible.

In addition to closing costs, you will also have some pre-paid items that consist of any per diem or daily interest due on the loan at closing and the initial deposits into your escrow account for the payment of property taxes, homeowner's insurance and private mortgage insurance.

The amount of pre-paid items collected will vary based on the time of year your loan closes and the pro-rated amounts due from the seller at closing. Because tax payment requirements vary in each state, your mortgage professional, real estate professional or escrow agent can help explain what amounts are required.

You will also receive a Truth-in-Lending Disclosure Statement (TIL) within three business days of your credit application. The truth-in-lending disclosure is one of the most important forms in the entire mortgage process. This form is required by RESPA (Real Estate Settlement Procedures Act) and was designed to show the total cost of your mortgage over the life of the loan based on the fees and terms of the particular loan. It contains such items as:

- Amount financed
- Annual percentage rate or APR

- Finance charge
- Payment schedule

The annual percentage rate (APR) is the total yearly cost of a mortgage stated as a percentage of the loan amount. Its primary purpose is to assist you in price comparison and includes the base interest rate, private mortgage insurance and certain lender fees. Some "Junk Fees" may not be included in the APR calculation, so it is always best to do an individual line item review to determine all costs.

You've Made It: Closing Day

IT'S FINALLY ARRIVED. Your loan has received final approval, the house passed inspection, and you're all packed up and ready to move. So what happens now?

Your closing is a meeting of all the parties involved in the transaction. Here, the final loan documents are signed along with the deeds and documents needed to legally transfer the property to you. Once all documents have been signed, and recorded with the county authority, you will be given the keys to your new home.

Your real estate agent, the escrow officer and/or closing agent, and your mortgage broker should all attend the closing appointment. I attended all of my closings to ensure that all of the loan documents were accurate prior to my borrower signing them. When you're in the interview process, remember to ask if your mortgage broker attends their closings. It's another step to protect your financial interests. Many brokers do not attend closings, and that can create unnecessary problems for the borrower.

People simply make typographical mistakes. I can't tell you how many times I have caught an error in the loan documents prior to signing and solved the problem for my borrower . . . before it ever became a problem.

The one thing you will probably remember most years after the closing is how many times you had to sign your name. There are a lot of documents in this process. Let's review some of what you can expect to sign during your closing appointment.

You will sign a form accepting the terms of the mortgage from the lender. In some states you will sign a mortgage instrument, and in other states you will sign a deed of trust.

You will also sign a mortgage note, which is your promise to repay the home loan in its entirety under the terms listed in the note. The note will include the interest rate, loan term, the monthly payment and dates due, as well as the place where the payments are to be sent.

Your lender will transfer the funds to escrow and instruct the escrow officer how to disburse the funds to the seller and the other appropriate parties. The seller signs a document called a deed, transferring the property to you.

The title company will make sure that all documents are signed, notarized, and recorded with the county recorder's office or appropriate authority.

There will also be other affidavits and declarations for you to sign. Affidavits and declarations are statements declaring something to be true. Some of these will include: the fact that your property will be your principal residence, a statement indicating that all repairs have been completed, or you accept the property in "as is" condition.

Make sure that you understand what you're signing. Never let anyone pressure you to hurry or sign something that you do not clearly understand. It is important to read the documents carefully.

Never hesitate to ask questions, you're the one financially responsible for this obligation. Rely on the expertise around the room to ensure that everything about the documents is clear and understood by all parties.

Once you've signed the last document, congratulations are in order—YOU ARE OFFICIALLY A HOMEOWNER!

Understanding Private Mortgage Insurance

PRIVATE MORTGAGE INSURANCE (PMI) offers protection for the lender in the case of default by the borrower. If you have less than 20% down payment on a conventional loan, private mortgage insurance is a requirement.

Private mortgage insurance costs vary by the amount of down payment, risk to the lender, loan term, credit score, and program type. Some plans offer up-front or all-in-one premium plans, while some plans allow you to finance it over the life of the loan. You can also be required to pay it monthly. I am not a big advocate of the upfront premium because it can increase your out-of-pocket cash requirements significantly.

Let's review an example loan scenario to give you a better understanding of how these rates are calculated. The following is an example of the monthly premium factors for a conventional loan based on down payment and a 30-year or 15-year fixed rate loan with a 720 or higher credit score. These numbers were pulled from a chart in 2011 and are not representative of current market factors.

Loan to value	30-year	15-year
95 - 97%	.88	.88
90.01 - 95%	.67	.62
85.01 - 90%	.49	.39
80.01 - 85%	.32	.30

Using our example above, let's calculate a $100,000 loan with a 7% down payment. That's a 93% loan to value, and the premium would be .67% of the loan amount.

$100,000 x .67% ($670.00) divided by 12 = $55.83

So our monthly premium would be $55.83 for private mortgage insurance. With the financed plan, the loan amount is increased to cover this premium—which can be as much as 3.8%—and/or the interest rate is increased to cover the cost. Using this option, you are paying interest on the mortgage insurance premium over the entire life of the loan, which may not be cost effective.

In my opinion, the monthly plan will be the best option for most borrowers on a conventional loan. You pay it monthly as required, but have the option of cancelling the private mortgage insurance requirement when the property value reaches 80% or less. That way, you are not paying any longer than necessary.

Dropping the PMI coverage is at the discretion of the lender, but in most cases, the lender will not automatically drop the coverage. In order to have your PMI coverage cancelled, you must meet the following general requirements:

- You must request the cancellation in writing.
- You must occupy the property as your principal residence.

- You have not been thirty days late or delinquent in the last two years of payment history.
- If you made improvements to the property, you must wait the minimum two-year waiting period to reflect good paying habits and provide a new appraisal showing an 80% or less loan to value.
- If you have not made improvements to the property, you can apply for cancellation if you pay the loan down to 80% loan to value based on the original loan amount.
- You may also apply for cancellation after five years, if the current appraised value supports a loan to value of 80% or less.

In today's mortgage environment, a request to cancel PMI is going to require a current appraisal. The lender will not allow you to pick the appraiser, but in most cases will order it for you. Don't go out and order your own appraisal or you may waste $400 and accomplish nothing. Submit your cancellation request to the lender, and then follow the steps as directed by them.

Do You Need a Home Inspection?

OBTAINING A HOME INSPECTION can be one of the most important things that you can do to make sure your home is in good condition. An authorized inspector will check all of the major components of the house, including such items as:

- Heating and cooling systems
- The plumbing
- The electrical system
- The roof
- The siding
- Walls, ceiling, floors
- The foundation, basement, and crawl space areas
- Built-in appliances
- and much more...

Make sure that the home inspector you use is a certified member of the National Institute of Building Inspectors. Members of NIBI are required to re-certify every year and stay current on construction and building code requirements.

Shop around, ask for referrals, and choose an inspector that you feel comfortable with. Missed items or costly repairs down the road can be devastating.

It's too important of an issue to rely on relatives or your construction friends to give you adequate information.

The Responsibilities of Home Ownership

BUYING A HOME is usually one of the biggest dreams we have as adults. But signing and closing on a mortgage loan is really just the beginning of your homeowner responsibilities.

It's always important to factor into your life the unpredictable or unexpected things that can show up and sometimes blindside you if you are not prepared. Items such as:

- A sudden illness or family emergency
- A loss of job
- Change in your family or relationship status

We all know these types of things can limit your ability to pay your financial obligations and mortgage payment on time. Making late payments results in late fees and will negatively affect your credit in the future.

It's important to always have a back-up plan to handle these types of financial headaches. Having an emergency bank account will give you the confidence that you can handle anything that comes your way.

The best idea is to work toward establishing three to six months of living expenses in a separate account. This keeps you from racking up credit card expenses and paying more interest in the end. Interest rates on credit cards can be high and making only minimum payments can cause long-term chaos in your overall financial goals.

Remember to budget for routine maintenance and repairs, also taking into account increases on homeowner's insurance and taxes. Think about areas where you can reduce non-essential spending or services to help decrease monthly expenses when needed.

Every precaution you take now will benefit you and your family in the future. It's also important to continually maintain your home for the comfort and safety of your family. When you're prepared, you will rarely be caught in any financial storm that may come your way.

Home Equity Loans or Lines of Credit

Another option to help out with unexpected expenses, besides an emergency account or your credit cards, can be a home equity loan or line of credit, also known as a HELOC.

Home equity products can be an excellent financial tool to help finance home improvements. They should not be used primarily for debt consolidation or other purposes, unless recommended by your tax professional.

The lender will determine a maximum credit line amount, and you make payments and pay interest only on the amount of credit that you have used. The lender will usually issue convenience checks for use in making draws on your credit line account.

Terms of these loans will usually include interest only payments for a pre-determined period of time (for example ten years). After this time, the draw option is removed and the principal-plus-interest payments are required if the loan is not paid in full at that time.

A HELOC is a revolving line of credit with an adjustable rate that is typically based on prime rate. With a HELOC, your home is used as collateral and will be secured by placing a second mortgage or a credit line deed of trust against your home.

Having a second mortgage or HELOC can make it difficult to refinance your first mortgage should you decide to do that later. Keep this in mind when determining if a HELOC is a good option for you.

Most lenders will allow you to borrow up to 85% of your home's value, but I have found that in the current mortgage environment, finding a lender for this type of loan can be a challenge. With soft markets, declining property values and other economic factors, lenders are taking a very critical look at approving a HELOC and will require a current appraisal.

When shopping for a HELOC look for the following features:

- No application, closing, account maintenance or check writing fees.
- A variable APR equal to prime rate with a low cap on interest rate increases.
- The ability to convert the HELOC or the portion used to a fixed rate loan to help protect against interest rate increases.
- No restrictions on principal repayment or penalties for early payoff.

Homeowners with good credit should be able to find a HELOC with most of these features.

There can be tax consequences when having a HELOC or Home Equity Loan. You may be able to deduct at least some of the interest you pay, but you should check with your tax professional to find out how you will be affected.

What a Realtor® Knows that You Don't

MY TOP PRODUCING AND MOST EXPERIENCED Realtor® colleagues sat down with me for some informal interviews while I was writing this book.

These are the professionals that I respect and trust most in the local real estate market. From these interviews, I identified the top three reasons why you should utilize the services of a licensed Realtor®.

#1: Knowledge of the market.

A full-time Realtor will be out in the neighborhoods each and every day. They are going to be familiar with area development, potential zoning issues and other neighborhood factors that can affect the livability of the property.

Being a member of the local multiple listing service (MLS), they have at their fingertips all of the information needed regarding possible property features to match with an individual client's needs.

Appointments to view the properties can be easily accomplished, along with providing information about comparable home sales in the same neighborhood. This type of information has unlimited value when making an offer and ensuring that every client is paying a fair price for their home.

#2: Understanding of Paperwork

Years ago, there was a one-page real estate purchase agreement. Today, the standard real estate purchase agreement is around ten pages in length.

Along with that, there are various addendums, agency forms, disclosures, and much more that must be completed in order to submit an offer on a home.

It's vitally important that these documents are completed correctly and your Realtor® will have built-in safe guards to protect both clients throughout the transaction.

#3: Ongoing Continuity

Your Realtor® has the ability to see the transaction through from start to finish. They must not only be able to find their client a nice home and complete the paper work properly, but also deal with the listing broker (seller's broker) to make sure the transaction goes as planned.

Realtors® abide by a strict code of ethics and can easily guide you through all the technical aspects of the offer process. Working with your mortgage professional, home inspector, escrow officer, negotiating repairs, managing potential appraisal issues, and coordinating closing are all part of the services they provide.

Need I say more about placing your next home purchase in the hands of a skilled Realtor®?

Building Your Custom Home from the Ground Up

BUILDING YOUR DREAM HOME can be a very big decision. Whether you own land now and want to build your dream home, or if you purchase a land/home package from a builder, getting a good value for your investment is critical.

This means choosing an established and reputable licensed builder you can trust, one who has the technical skills and knowledge to build a good home while being fair and professional.

Before you enter into any legal agreement, it is important to do your homework. Ask for references, make sure that the builder is appropriately licensed with the state and/or local authority and has no claims or disputes filed against them. Membership in a state or local builders association is an indication of a their ongoing commitment to excellence and professionalism.

Just like it is important to interview your mortgage professional, it is also vitally important to interview your builder. Here is a list of questions to ask:

- Are you a state or local builders association member?
- How many homes have you built in the last three years?

- How many homes are you expecting to build this year?
- How long does it take to complete a home that is similar to the one that we want to build? Always ask about permits and weather factors. Does the builder appear confident and realistic?
- Can you show me samples of your work?
- Do we need to get construction financing or do we pay for the home when it's complete?
- Can you provide references? Who do you bank with? May I call them for a reference?
- Are the other homes that you currently have under contract on schedule to be completed on time?
- Are we allowed to visit the construction site during construction?
- How do you handle problems after construction is completed?
- Do you offer a warranty with our new home?

These questions are important because you want to see the builder's quality, experience and service performance in the past. This will also help provide you with some ideas when planning the look of your new dream home.

It's hard to get what you want if you don't ask for it, so don't hesitate to speak your mind! Always balance price and value as you work to build the home of your dreams.

If the builder or sales agent isn't responsive to your questions, it's time to keep shopping.

Loan Processing Checklist

THE FOLLOWING ITEMS may be critical to your loan being completed in a timely manner. Please provide them to your mortgage professional at application, if they apply to you.

- ○ Last thirty days paycheck stubs for all borrowers
- ○ Last two years W-2s for all borrowers
- ○ Last two years federal tax returns for all borrowers (including schedules)
- ○ Last two months of bank statements (checking, savings and investment/retirement)
- ○ Copy of divorce decree, including all pages, if applicable
- ○ Copy of bankruptcy discharge papers, if applicable
- ○ Explanation letter (for late payments, collections, etc.)
- ○ Copy of driver's license for all borrowers
- ○ Copy of all pension statements or award letters, etc.
- ○ Copy of social security annual award letter, statement, etc.
- ○ Copy of accepted purchase agreement (when property is selected)

Uniform Residential Loan Application

Complete a Uniform Residential Loan Application prior to visiting and interviewing your mortgage professional. Utilizing this form along with the **Loan Processing Checklist** will help you get prepared prior to submitting an actual application.

If there are any areas that you do not understand, leave those items blank and a mortgage professional can help you complete them.

To obtain an offical Uniform Residential Loan Application (FNMA Form 1003) go to:

https://www.efanniemae.com/sf/formsdocs/forms/pdf/sellingtrans/1003.pdf

Sample Gift Letter Form/Certification

Date Created

To Whom It May Concern:

I (NAME OF DONOR/s) am the (RELATIONSHIP TO APPLICANT) of (NAME OF APPLICANT/s), and am giving the sum of (AMOUNT GIVEN) as a gift for the purchase of (SUBJECT PROPERTY ADDRESS).

This is a gift and no repayment is expected or implied. I also understand that proof of evidence may be required in the form of bank statements, stock statements or other source to demonstrate the ability to give the gift. The source of funds for the gift is (NAME OF INSTITUTION) and will be in the form of a (SELECT ONE: Electronic Transfer / Cashier's Check / Personal Check). This cash gift was/will be transferred to the applicant on (DATE OF FUNDS TRANSFER).

The funds given to the applicant were not made available to the donor from any person or entity with an interest in the state of the property, including the seller, real estate agent, broker, builder, loan officer or any entity associated with them.

(DONOR'S SIGNATURE/s) and (DATE SIGNED)

DONOR'S ADDRESS
CITY, STATE, ZIP

(APPLICANT'S SIGNATURE/s) and (DATE SIGNED)

I/We fully understand that it is a Federal crime punishable by fine or imprisonment, or both, to knowingly make any false statements when applying for this mortgage, as applicable under the provision of Title 18, United States Code, Section 1014 and Section 1010.

Resource Websites

http://www.karensimpsonhankins.com

http://www.annualcreditreport.com

http://www.va.gov

http://www.hud.gov

http://www.fanniemae.com/homebuyers/homepath/index.jhtml

http://www.fha.gov

http://www.namb.org

http://www.nmlsconsumeraccess.org

Glossary of Important Terms

-A-

Abstract (of Title): A summary of the public records relating to the title of a particular piece of land. An attorney or title insurance company reviews an abstract of title to determine whether there are any title defects which must be cleared before a buyer can purchase.

Acceleration Clause: Condition in a mortgage that may require the balance of the loan to become due immediately if regular mortgage payments are not made or for breach of other conditions of the mortgage.

Accepted Purchase Agreement: A purchase agreement that is fully signed and accepted by both buyer and seller with mutual consent to enter into a contract and be bound by the terms of the offer.

Additional Principal Payment: A payment by a borrower of more than the scheduled principal amount due in order to reduce the remaining balance on the loan.

Adjustable Rate Mortgage: (ARM) A mortgage in which the interest rate is adjusted periodically according to the movement in a pre-selected index.

Adjustment Date: The date on which the interest rate changes for an adjustable rate mortgage.

Adjustment Period: For an adjustable rate mortgage, the time between changes in the interest rate charged. The most common adjustment intervals are one, three or five years.

Agreement of Sale: Also known by various names such as contract of purchase, purchase agreement, or sales agreement according to location or jurisdiction. A contract in which a seller agrees to sell and a buyer agrees to buy under certain specific terms and conditions spelled out in writing and signed by both parties.

Amenities: Features of real property that enhances its attractiveness and increases the occupant's or user's satisfaction although the feature is not essential to the property's use. Natural amenities include a pleasant or desirable location near water, scenic views of the surrounding area, etc. Human-made amenities include swimming pools, tennis courts, community buildings and other recreational facilities.

Amortize: Reduce a debt by regular payments of both principal and interest.

Amortization: A payment plan that enables the borrower to reduce his debt gradually through monthly payments of principal.

Amortization Schedule: A timetable for repayment of a mortgage loan. An amortization schedule shows the amount of each payment applied to interest and principal and shows the remaining balance after each payment is made.

Amortization Term: The amount of time required to amortize the mortgage loan. The amortization term is expressed as a number of months.

Annual Percentage Rate: (APR) The total yearly cost of a mortgage stated as a percentage of the loan amount that includes the base interest rate, primary mortgage insurance and loan origination fee (points).

Application: A form used to apply for a mortgage loan and to record pertinent information concerning a prospective mortgagor and the proposed security.

Application Fee: The fee charged by the lender to the borrower for applying for a loan.

Appraised Value: An opinion of a property's fair market value, based on an appraiser's knowledge, experience, and analysis of the property.

Appraiser: A person qualified by education, training, and experience to estimate the value of real property and personal property.

Appraisal: A professional opinion of the market value of a property.

Appreciation: An increase in the value of a house due to changes in market conditions or other causes.

Assessed Value: the valuation placed upon property by a public tax assessor for purposes of taxation.

Assessment: The process of placing a value on property for the strict purpose of taxation. May also refer to a levy against property for a special purpose, such as a sewer assessment.

Assessor: A public official who establishes the value of a property for taxation purposes.

Asset: Anything of monetary value that is owned by a person. Assets include real property, personal property, and enforceable claims against others (including bank accounts, stocks, mutual funds, and so on).

Assignment: The transfer of a mortgage from one person to another.

Assumable Loan: These loans may be passed on from a seller of a home to the buyer. The buyer "assumes" all outstanding payments.

Assumption Clause: A provision in an assumable mortgage that allows a buyer to assume responsibility for the mortgage from the seller. The loan does not need to be paid in full by the original borrower upon sale or transfer of the property.

Assumption Fee: The fee paid to a lender (usually by the purchaser of real property) resulting from the assumption of an existing mortgage.

Assumption of Mortgage: An obligation undertaken by the purchaser of property to be personally liable for payment of an existing mortgage. In an assumption, the purchaser is substituted for the original mortgagor in the mortgage instrument and the original mortgagor is to be released from further liability in the assumption, the mortgagee's consent is usually required.

Attorney-in-fact: One who holds a power of attorney from another to execute documents on behalf of the grantor of the power. Most lenders will require a Specific Power-of-attorney Form.

- B -

Balance Sheet: A financial statement that shows assets, liabilities, and net worth as of a specific date.

Bankruptcy: A proceeding in a federal court in which a debtor who owes more than his or her assets can relieve the debts by transferring his or her assets to a trustee.

Beneficiary: The person designated to receive the income from a trust, estate, or a deed of trust.

Bill of Sale: A written document that transfers title to personal property.

Binder: Also referred to as an Offer to Purchase. A preliminary agreement, secured by the payment of earnest money, between a buyer and seller as an offer to purchase real estate. A binder secures the right to purchase real estate upon agreed terms for a limited period of time. If the buyer changes his mind or is unable to purchase, the earnest money is forfeited unless the binder expressly provides that it is to be refunded.

Broker: See Real Estate Broker.

Blanket Insurance Policy: A single policy that covers more than one piece of property (or more than one person).

Bond: An interest-bearing certificate of debt with a maturity date. An obligation of a government or business corporation. A real estate bond is a written obligation usually secured by a mortgage or a deed of trust.

Borrower: One who receives funds with the expressed or implied intention of repaying the loan in full.

Bridge Loan: A form of second trust that is collateralized by the borrower's present home (which is usually for sale) in a manner that allows the proceeds to be used for closing on a new house before the present home is sold.

Broker: An individual in the business of assisting in arranging funding or negotiating contracts for a client but who does not loan the money himself. Brokers usually charge a fee or receive a commission for their services.

Building Code: Local regulations that control design, construction, and materials used in construction. Building codes are based on safety and health standards.

Building Line or Setback: Distances from the ends and/or sides of the lot beyond which construction may not extend. The building line may be established by a filed plat of subdivision, by restrictive covenants in deeds or leases, by building codes, or by zoning ordinances.

Buy Down: Money advanced by an individual (seller, builder, etc.) to reduce monthly payments for a home mortgage either during the entire term or for an initial period of years.

- C -

Call option: A provision in the mortgage that gives the mortgagee the right to call the mortgage due and payable at the end of a specified period for whatever reason.

Cap: A provision of an ARM limiting how much the interest rate or mortgage payments may increase.

Cash-out Refinance: A refinance transaction in which the amount of money received from the new loan exceeds the total of the money needed to repay the existing first mortgage, closing costs, points, and the amount required to satisfy any outstanding subordinate mortgage liens.

Certificate of Eligibility: A document issued by the federal government certifying a veteran's eligibility for a Department of Veterans Affairs (VA) mortgage. Certificate of Reasonable Value (CRV) A document issued by the Department of Veterans Affairs (VA) that establishes the maximum value and loan amount for a VA mortgage.

Certificate of Title: A certificate issued by a title company or a written opinion rendered by an attorney that the seller has good marketable and insurable title to the property, which he is offering for sale. A certificate of title offers no protection against any hidden defects in the title, which an examination of the records could not reveal. The issuer of a certificate of title is liable only for damages due to negligence. The protection offered a homeowner under a certificate of title is not as great as that offered in a title insurance policy.

Chain of Title: The history of all of the documents that transfer title to a parcel of real property, starting with the earliest existing document and ending with the most recent.

Clear Title: A title that is free of liens or legal questions as to ownership of the property

Closing: The occasion where a sale is finalized; the buyer signs the mortgage, and closing costs are paid. Also called "settlement."

Closing Costs: Expenses (over and above the price of the property) incurred by buyers and sellers in transferring ownership of a property. Also called "settlement costs."

Cloud (on Title): An outstanding claim or encumbrance, which adversely affects the marketability of title.

Co-Borrower: An additional borrower on a loan. A co-borrower's obligation on a loan are the same as all other borrowers.

Coinsurance Clause: A provision in a hazard insurance policy that states the amount of coverage that must be maintained -- as a percentage of the total value of the property -- for the insured to collect the full amount of a loss.

Collateral: An asset (such as a car or a home) that guarantees the repayment of a loan. The borrower risks losing the asset if the loan is not repaid according to the terms of the loan contract.

Collection: The efforts used to bring a delinquent mortgage current and to file the necessary notices to proceed with foreclosure when necessary.

Co-maker: A person who signs a promissory note along with the borrower. A co-maker's signature guarantees that the loan will be repaid, because the borrower and the co-maker are equally responsible for the repayment.

Commission: Money paid to a real estate agent or broker by the seller as compensation for finding a buyer and completing the sale.

Commitment Letter: A formal offer by a lender stating the terms under which it agrees to loan money to a homebuyer.

Common Area Assessments: Levies against individual unit owners in a condominium or planned unit development (PUD) project for additional capital to defray homeowners' association costs and expenses and to repair, replace, maintain, improve, or operate the common areas of the project.

Common Areas: Those portions of a building, land, and amenities owned (or managed) by a planned unit development (PUD) or condominium project's homeowners' association (or a cooperative project's cooperative corporation) that are used by all of the unit owners, who share in the common expenses of their operation and maintenance. Common areas include swimming pools, tennis courts, and other recreational facilities, as well as common corridors of buildings, parking areas, means of ingress and egress, etc.

Community Property: In some western and southwestern states, a form of ownership under which property acquired during a marriage is presumed to be owned jointly unless acquired as separate property of either spouse.

Comparable: An abbreviation for comparable properties used for comparative purposes in the appraisal process; facilities of reasonably the same size and location with similar amenities; properties which have been recently sold, which have characteristics similar to property under consideration, thereby indicating the approximate fair market value of the subject property.

Condominium: Individual ownership of a dwelling unit and an individual interest in the common areas and facilities, which serve the multi-unit project.

Construction Loan: A short-term loan for funding the cost of construction. The lender advances funds to the builder as the work progresses.

Consumer Reporting Agency: An organization that prepares reports that are used by lenders to determine a potential borrower's credit history. The agency obtains data for these reports from a credit repository as well as from other sources.

Contingency: A condition that must be met before a contract is legally binding.

Contract: An oral or written agreement to do or not to do a certain thing.

Contractor: In the construction industry, a contractor is one who contracts to erect buildings or portions of them. There are also contractors for each phase of construction: heating, electrical, plumbing, air conditioning, road building, bridge and dam erection, and others.

Conventional Mortgage: Any mortgage that is not insured or guaranteed by the federal government.

Convertibility Clause: A provision in some adjustable-rate mortgages (ARMS) that allows the borrower to change the ARM to a fixed-rate mortgage at specified time.

Convertible Arm: An adjustable-rate mortgage that can be converted to a fixed-rate mortgage under specified conditions.

Cost of Funds Index: (COFI) An index that is used to determine interest rate changes for certain adjustable-rate mortgage (ARM) plans. It represents the weighted-average cost of savings, borrowings, and advances of the 11th District members of the Federal Home Loan Bank of San Francisco.

Covenant: A clause in a mortgage that obligates or restricts the borrower and that, if violated, can result in foreclosure.

Commitment: A written letter of agreement detailing the terms and conditions by which the lender will lend and the borrower will borrow funds to finance a home.

Credit Approval Letter: A written letter of agreement detailing the terms and conditions of a Pre-approval by a lender subject to a satisfactory property being submitted to a lender. Also, known as a Pre-approval Letter.

Credit History: A record of an individual's open and fully repaid debts. A credit history helps a lender to determine whether a potential borrower has a history of repaying debts in a timely manner.

Credit Life Insurance: A type of insurance often bought by mortgagors because it will pay off the mortgage debt if the mortgagor dies while the policy is in force.

Creditor: A person to whom money is owed.

Credit Report: A report of an individual's credit history prepared by a credit bureau and used by a lender in determining a loan applicant's creditworthiness.

Credit Repository: An organization that gathers, records, updates, and stores financial and public records information about the payment records of individuals who are being considered for credit. Also, known as a Credit Reporting Agency (CRA).

-D-

Deed of Trust: Like a mortgage, a security instrument whereby real property is given as security for a debt. However, in a deed of trust there are three parties to the instrument: the borrower, the trustee, and the lender, (or beneficiary). In such a transaction, the borrower transfers the legal title for the property to the trustee who holds the property in trust as security for the payment of the debt to the lender or beneficiary. If the borrower pays the debt as agreed, the deed of trust becomes void. If, however, he defaults in the payment of the debt, the trustee may sell the property at a public sale, under the terms of the deed of trust. In most jurisdictions where the deed of trust is in force, the borrower is subject to having his property sold without benefit of legal proceedings. A few States have begun in recent years to treat the deed of trust like a mortgage.

Default: Failure to make mortgage payments on a timely basis or to comply with other conditions of a mortgage.

Deposit: A sum of money given to bind the sale of real estate, or a sum of money given to ensure payment or an advance of funds in the processing of a loan.

Depreciation: A decline in the value of property; the opposite of "appreciation."

Discount Points: See Points.

Documentary Stamps: A state tax, in the forms of stamps, required on deeds and mortgages when real estate title passes from one owner to another. The amount of stamps required varies with each State.

Down Payment: The part of the purchase price, which the buyer pays in cash and does not finance with a mortgage

Due-on-sale Provision: A provision in a mortgage that allows the lender to demand repayment in full if the borrower sells the property that serves as security for the mortgage.

Due-on-transfer Provision: This terminology is usually used for second mortgages.

- E -

Earnest Money: The deposit money given to the seller or his agent by the potential buyer upon the signing of the agreement of sale to show that he is serious about buying the house. If the sale goes through, the earnest money is applied against the down payment. If the sale does not go through, the earnest money will be forfeited or lost unless the binder or offer to purchase expressly provides that it is refundable.

Easement Rights: A right-of-way granted to a person or company authorizing access to or over the owner's land. An electric company obtaining a right-of-way across private property is a common example.

Effective Age: An appraiser's estimate of the physical condition of a building. The actual age of a building may be shorter or longer than its effective age.

Effective Gross Income: Normal annual income including overtime that is regular or guaranteed. The income may be from more than one source. Salary is generally the principal source, but other income may qualify if it is significant and stable.

Encumbrance: A legal right or interest in land that affects a good or clear title, and diminishes the land's value. It can take numerous forms, such as zoning ordinances, easement rights, claims, mortgages, liens, charges, a pending legal action, unpaid taxes, or restrictive covenants. An encumbrance does not legally prevent transfer of the property to another. A title search is all that is usually done to reveal the existence of such encum brances, and it is up to the buyer to determine whether he wants to purchase with the encumbrance, or what can be done to remove it.

Equal Credit Opportunity Act: (ECOA) A federal law that requires lenders and other creditors to make credit equally available without discrimination based on race, color, religion, national origin, age, sex, marital status, or receipt of income from public assistance programs.

Equity: The difference between the market value of a property and the homeowner's outstanding mortgage balance.

Equity Loan: A loan based on the borrower's equity in his or her home. Prior to closing; also, an account held by the lender into which a homeowner pays money for taxes and insurance.

Escrow Account: The account in which a mortgage servicer holds the borrower's escrow payments prior to paying property expenses.

Escrow Analysis: The periodic examination of escrow accounts to determine if current monthly deposits will provide sufficient funds to pay taxes, insurance, and other bills when due.

Escrow Disbursements: The use of escrow funds to pay real estate taxes, hazard insurance, mortgage insurance, and other property expenses as they become due.

Escrow Payment: The portion of a mortgagor's monthly payment that is held by the servicer to pay for taxes, hazard insurance, mortgage insurance, lease payments, and other items as they become due.

Examination of Title: The report on the title of a property from the public records or an abstract of the title.

Exclusive Listing: A written contract that gives a licensed real estate agent the exclusive right to sell a property for a specified time, but reserving the owner's right to sell the property alone without the payment of a commission.

- F -

Fair Credit Reporting Act: A consumer protection law that regulates the disclosure of consumer credit reports by consumer/credit reporting agencies and establishes procedures for correcting mistakes on one's credit record.

Fair-market-value: The highest price that a buyer, willing but not compelled to buy would pay, and the lowest a seller, willing but not compelled to sell, would accept.

Federal Deposit Insurance Corporation: (FDIC) Provides insurance of accounts for institutions whose deposits were formerly covered by the Federal Savings & Loan Insurance Corporation. (FSLIC).

Fee Simple: The greatest possible interest a person can have in real estate.

Fee Simple Estate: An unconditional, unlimited estate of inheritance that represents the greatest estate and most extensive interest in land that can be enjoyed. It is of perpetual duration. When the real estate is in a condominium project, the unit owner is the exclusive owner only of the air space within his or her portion of the building (the unit) and is an owner in common with respect to the land and other common portions of the property.

Federal Housing Administration: (FHA) A division of the Department of Housing and Urban Development. The FHA's main activity is the insuring of residential mortgage loans made by private lenders. It sets standards for construction and underwriting. FHA neither lends money, nor plans, nor constructs housing.

FHA Loan: Government loans are loans that are guaranteed or purchased by government organizations. Two of the most popular Government Loans are the Federal Housing Administration (FHA) and the Department of Veterans Affairs (VA).

Federal Home Loan Mortgage Corporation, Freddie Mac: (FHLMC) A private corporation authorized by Congress, which became an independent, stockholder-owned government corporation with the passage of FIRREA. FHLMC promotes the flow of funds into the housing markets by purchasing conventional mortgages in the secondary market and selling securities backed by those mortgages in the capital market.

Finance Charge: The total dollar amount your loan will cost you. It includes all interest payments for the life of the loan, any interest paid at closing, your origination fee and any other charges paid to the lender and/or broker. Appraisal, credit report and title search fees are not included in the finance charge calculation.

Firm Commitment: A lender's agreement to make a loan to a specific borrower on a specific property.

First Mortgage: The mortgage that has first claim in the event of default.

Fixed Installment: The monthly payment due on a mortgage loan.

Fixed-Rate Mortgage: (FRM) A mortgage in which the interest rate does not change during the entire term of the loan.

Federal National Mortgage Association, Fannie Mae: (FNMA) A government-sponsored corporation, owned solely by private investors, created to provide support to the secondary market for FHA and VA mortgages and conventional mortgages.

Flood Insurance: Insurance that compensates for physical property damage resulting from flooding. It is required for properties located in federally designated flood areas.

Forfeiture: The loss of money, property, rights, or privileges due to a breach of legal obligation.

Foreclosure: The process by which a mortgage property may be sold when a mortgage is in default.

Fully Amortized ARM: An adjustable-rate mortgage (ARM) with a monthly payment that is sufficient to amortize the remaining balance, at the interest accrual rate, over the amortization term.

Full Recasting: Setting the P&I payments to the level that will fully amortize the loan's outstanding balance over the remaining term using the fully indexed accrual rate at the recasting point.

Fully Indexed Accrual Rate: The interest (accrual) rate resulting from the index at closing (or at another point in the loan) plus the lender's full spread, rounded as prescribed in the loan documents (often to the nearest 1/8th of 1%).

- G -

General Warranty Deed: A deed which conveys not only all the grantor's interests in and title to the property to the grantee, but also warrants that if the title is defective or has a "cloud" on it (such as mortgage claims, tax liens, title claims, judgments, or mechanic's liens against it) the grantee may hold the grantor liable.

Good Faith Estimate: An estimate of charges, which a borrower is likely to incur in connection with a loan closing.

Government Loans FHA/VA: Government loans are loans that are guaranteed or purchased by government organizations. Two of the most popular Government Loans are the Federal Housing Administration (FHA) and the Department of Veterans Affairs (VA).

Graduated Payment Mortgage: (GPM) A mortgage where the payments are scheduled to increase, usually annually, for a set number of years, and then level off. GPM can be used with either a fixed or adjustable interest rate, and usually has a 30-year term.

Grantee: The party in the deed who is the buyer or recipient.

Grantor: The party in the deed who is the seller or giver.

Gross Monthly Income: The total amount the borrower earns per month, not counting any taxes or expenses. Often used in calculations to determine whether a borrower qualifies for a particular loan.

Growing Equity Mortgage: (GEM) A fixed rate, graduated payment mortgage with small initial payments that increase each year so that the loan pays off in a shortened term, usually 15 years.

- H -

Hazard Insurance: Insurance to protect the homeowner and the lender against physical damage to a property from fire, wind, vandalism, or other hazards.

Home Equity Line of Credit: HELOC

Homeowner's Insurance: An insurance policy that combines liability coverage and hazard insurance.

Homeowner's Warranty: A type of insurance that covers repairs to specified parts of a house for a specific period of time.

Housing Ratio: The ratio of the monthly housing payment to total gross monthly income. Also called Payment-to-Income Ratio or Front-End Ratio.

Housing and Urban Development: (HUD) A cabinet department responsible for the implementation and administration of government housing and urban development programs.

HUD-1 Uniform Settlement Statement: A standard form that discloses the fees and services associated with the closing with your mortgage loan.

- I -

Income Property: Real estate developed or improved to produce income.

Index: Also referred to as a rate index. A regularly published rate, independent of the lending institution that measures the prevailing cost of funds, and is used periodically with the margin to set AML accrual rates.

Initial Borrower Interest Rate: The rate on which the borrower's first payment is calculated.

Initial Borrower Payment Rate: The annual interest rate used to calculate the borrower's initial cash payment.

Inflation: An increase in the amount of money or credit available in relation to the amount of goods or services available, which causes an increase in the general price level of goods and services. Over time, inflation reduces the purchasing power of a dollar, making it worth less.

Initial Interest Rate: The original interest rate of the mortgage at the time of closing.

Installment: The regular periodic payment that a borrower agrees to make to a lender.

Installment Loan: Borrowed money that is repaid in equal payments, known as installments. A furniture loan is often paid for as an installment loan.

Insurable Title: A property title that a title insurance company agrees to insure against defects and disputes.

Insurance: A contract that provides compensation for specific losses in exchange for a periodic payment. An individual contract is known as an insurance policy, and the periodic payment is known as an insurance premium.

Insurance Binder: A document that states that insurance is temporarily in effect. Because the coverage will expire by a specified date, a permanent policy must be obtained before the expiration date.

Insured Mortgage: A mortgage that is protected by the Federal Housing Administration (FHA) or by private mortgage insurance (MI). If the borrower defaults on the loan, the insurer must pay the lender the lesser of the loss incurred or the insured amount

Interest: The fee charged for borrowing money.

Interest Accrual Rate: The percentage rate at which interest accrues on the mortgage. In most cases, it is also the rate used to calculate the monthly payments, although it is not used for an adjustable-rate mortgage (ARM) with payment change limitations.

Interest Rate: The percentage of an amount of money, which is paid for its use for a specified time.

Interest Rate Cap: A provision of an ARM limiting how much interest rates may increase per adjustment period.

Interest Rate Ceiling: For an adjustable-rate mortgage (ARM), the maximum interest rate, as specified in the mortgage note.

Interest Rate Floor: For an adjustable-rate mortgage (ARM), the minimum interest rate, as specified in the mortgage note.

Investment Property: A property that is not occupied by the owner.

Individual Retirement Account: (IRA) A retirement account that allows individuals to make tax-deferred contributions to a personal retirement fund. Individuals can place IRA funds in bank accounts or in other forms of investment such as stocks, bonds, or mutual funds.

- J -

Joint Tenancy: A form of co-ownership that gives each tenant equal interest and equal rights in the property, including the right of survivorship.

Judgment: A decision made by a court of law. In judgments that require the repayment of a debt, the court may place a lien against the debtor's real property as collateral for the judgment's creditor.

Judgment Lien: A lien on the property of a debtor resulting from the decree of a court.

Judicial Foreclosure: A type of foreclosure proceeding used in some states that is handled as a civil lawsuit and conducted entirely under the auspices of a court.

Jumbo Loans: Jumbo, or non-conforming, is a term used to describe a loan that does not conform to Fannie Mae or Freddie Mac guidelines.

- K -

- L -

Late Charge: The penalty a borrower must pay when a payment is made a stated number of days (usually 15) after the due date.

Lease: A written agreement between the property owner and a tenant that stipulates the conditions under which the tenant may possess the real estate for a specified period of time and rent.

Leasehold Estate: A way of holding title to a property wherein the mortgagor does not actually own the property but rather has a recorded long-term lease on it.

Legal Description: A property description, recognized by law that is sufficient to locate and identify the property without oral testimony.

Lender: An institution that makes loans to borrowers on real estate.

Liabilities: A person's financial obligations. Liabilities include long-term and short-term debt, as well as any other amounts that are owed to others.

Liability Insurance: Insurance coverage that offers protection against claims alleging that a property owner's negligence or inappropriate action resulted in bodily injury or property damage to another party.

Lien: A legal claim against a property that must be paid when the property is sold.

Lifetime Cap: A provision of an ARM that limits the total increase in interest rates over the life of the loan.

Lifetime Payment Cap: For an adjustable-rate mortgage (ARM), a limit on the amount that payments can increase or decrease over the life of the mortgage.

Line of Credit: An agreement by a commercial bank or other financial institution to extend credit up to a certain amount for a certain time to a specified borrower.

Liquid Asset: A cash asset or an asset that is easily converted into cash.

Loan: A sum of borrowed money (principal) that is generally repaid with interest.

Loan Commitment: Formal offer by a lender stating the terms under which it agrees to loan money to a homebuyer.

Loan Origination: The process by which a mortgage lender brings into existence a mortgage secured by real property.

Loan Servicing: The collection of mortgage payments from borrowers and related responsibilities of a loan servicer.

Loan-To-Value: (LTV) The loan-to-value ratio is the original loan amount divided by the lower of the sales price or the appraised value.

Lock: The period, expressed in days, during which a lender will guarantee a rate.

Lock-in Period: The time period during which the lender has guaranteed an interest rate to a borrower.

- M -

Marketable Title: A title that is free and clear of objectionable liens, clouds, or other title defects. A title which enables an owner to sell his property freely to others and which others will accept without objection.

Master Association: A homeowners' association in a large condominium or planned unit development (PUD) project that is made up of representatives from associations covering specific areas within the project. In effect, it is a "second-level" association that handles matters affecting the entire development, while the "first-level" associations handle matters affecting their particular portions of the project.

Maturity: The date on which the principal balance of a loan, bond, or other financial instrument becomes due and payable.

Merged Credit Report: A credit report that contains information from three credit repositories. When the report is created, the information is compared for duplicate entries. Any duplicates are combined to provide a summary of your credit.

Margin: Sometimes called the "spread"" The amount the lender adds to the index to determine the Fully Indexed Accrual Rate.

Money Market Account: A savings account that provides bank depositors with many of the advantages of a money market fund. Certain regulatory restrictions apply to the withdrawal of funds from a money market account.

Money Market Fund: A mutual fund that allows individuals to participate in managed investments in short-term debt securities, such as certificates of deposit and Treasury bills.

Monthly Housing Expense: Total principal, interest, taxes, and insurance paid by the borrower on a monthly basis. Used with gross income to determine affordability.

Monthly Payment Mortgage: A mortgage that requires payments to reduce the debt once a month.

Mortgage: A legal document that pledges a property to the lender as security for a payment of a debt.

Mortgage Banker: A company that originates mortgages exclusively for resale in the secondary market.

Mortgage Broker: A company that for a fee matches borrowers with lenders.

Mortgagee: The lender in a mortgage agreement.

Mortgage Commitment: A written notice from the bank or other lending institution saying it will advance mortgage funds in a specified amount to enable a buyer to purchase a house.

Mortgage Insurance Premium: The payment made by a borrower to the lender for transmittal to HUD to help defray the cost of the FHA mortgage insurance program and to provide a reserve fund to protect lenders against loss in insured mortgage transactions. In FHA insured mortgages this represents an annual rate of one-half of one percent paid by the mortgagor on a monthly basis.

Mortgage Life Insurance: A type of term life insurance often bought by mortgagors. The amount of coverage decreases as the principal balance declines. In the event that the borrower dies while the policy is in force, the debt is automatically satisfied by insurance proceeds.

Mortgage Note: A written agreement to repay a loan. The agreement is secured by a mortgage, serves as proof of indebtedness, and states the manner in which it shall be paid. The note states the actual amount of the debt that the mortgage secures and renders the mortgagor personally responsible for repayment.

Mortgagor: The borrower in a mortgage agreement.

Multi-dwelling Units: Properties that provide separate housing units for more than one family, although they secure only a single mortgage.

Multifamily Mortgage: A residential mortgage on a dwelling that is designed to house more than four families, such as a high-rise apartment complex.

- N -

Negative Amortization: Also called "Deferred Interest." A gradual increase in mortgage debt that occurs when the monthly payment is not large enough to cover the entire principal and interest due. The amount of the shortfall is added to the remaining balance to create "negative" amortization

Net Cash Flow: The income that remains for an investment property after the monthly operating income is reduced by the monthly housing expense, which includes principal, interest, taxes, and insurance (PITI) for the mortgage, homeowners' association dues, leasehold payments, and subordinate financing payments.

Net Effective Income: Gross income less federal income tax.

Net Worth: The value of all assets, including cash, less total liabilities.

No cash-out Refinance: A refinance transaction in which the new mortgage amount is limited to the sum of the remaining balance of the existing first mortgage, closing costs (including prepaid items), points, the amount required to satisfy any mortgage liens that are more than one year old (if the borrower chooses to satisfy them), and other funds for the borrower's use (as long as the amount does not exceed 1 percent of the principal amount of the new mortgage).

Non-liquid Asset: An asset that cannot easily be converted into cash.

Note: A legal document that obligates a borrower to repay a mortgage loan at a stated interest rate during a specified period of time.

Note Rate: The interest rate stated on a mortgage note.

Notice of Default: A formal written notice to a borrower that a default has occurred and that legal action may be taken.

- O -

Original Principal Balance: The total amount of principal owed on a mortgage before any payments are made.

Origination Fee: A fee paid to a lender for processing a loan Application.

Owner Financing: A property purchase transaction in which the property seller provides all or part of the financing.

Owner Occupied: Means the property is the owner's primary residence.

- P -

Payment Adjustment Period: The length of time (typically a year) between changes to the borrower's P&I (Principal & Interest) payment.

Payment Buy Down: Payment buy downs occur when a third party, typically a builder, pays part of the initial P&I payments for a year or two, so that the borrower has smaller payments and can qualify for the loan.

Payment Cap: A limit on the amount the payment can be changed at the end of each Payment Adjustment Period.

Payment Discount: In a payment discount, the lender reduces the first year's interest rate to make the mortgagor more attractive to borrowers.

Periodic Payment Cap: A limit on the amount that payments can increase or decrease during any one-adjustment period.

Periodic Rate Cap: A limit on the amount that the interest rate can increase or decrease during any one adjustment period, regardless of how high or low the index might be.

Personal Property: Any property that is not real property.

PITI: Principal, Interest, Taxes and Insurance are components of a mortgage payment.

Plat: A map or chart of a lot, subdivision or community drawn by a surveyor showing boundary lines, buildings, improvements on the land, and easements.

Points: A one-time charge by the lender to increase the yield of the loan; a point is 1 percent of the amount of the mortgage.

Power of Attorney: A legal document that authorizes another person to act on one's behalf. A power of attorney can grant complete authority or can be limited to certain acts and/or certain periods of time.

Prepayment Penalty: A penalty charged for payment of a mortgage loan, in whole or in part, prior to the due date, depending on how the penalty is assessed.

Pre-Qualification: The process of determining how much money a prospective homebuyer will be eligible to borrow before application.

Prime Rate: The interest rates that banks charge to their preferred customers.

Principal: The amount borrowed or remaining unpaid, also, that part of the monthly payment that reduces the outstanding balance of a mortgage.

Private Mortgage Insurance: Insurance provided by nongovernmental insurers that protect lenders against loss if a borrower defaults.

Promissory Note: A written promise to repay a specified amount over a specified period of time.

Public Auction: A meeting in an announced public location to sell property to repay a mortgage that is in default.

Planned Unit Development: (PUD) A project or subdivision that includes common property that is owned and maintained by a homeowners' association for the benefit and use of the individual PUD unit owners.

Purchase Agreement: See Agreement of Sale

Purchase Money Transaction: The acquisition of property through the payment of money or its equivalent.

- Q -

Qualifying Ratios: Guidelines applied by lenders to determine how large a loan to grant a homebuyer.

Quitclaim Deed: A deed, which transfers whatever interest, the maker of the deed may have in the particular parcel of land. A quitclaim deed is often given to clear the title when the grantor's interest in a property is questionable. By accepting such a deed the buyer assumes all the risks. Such a deed makes no warranties as to the title, but simply transfers to the buyer whatever interest the grantor has. (See deed.)

- R -

Rate Caps: Also referred "Interest Rate Caps." A limit on the amount of which the interest rate charged to the borrower can be changed.

Rate Lock: A commitment issued by a lender to a borrower or other mortgage originator guaranteeing a specified interest rate for a specified period of time.

Real Estate Broker: A middleman or agent who buys and sells real estate for a company, firm, or individual on a commission basis. The broker does not have title to the property, but generally represents the owner.

Real Estate Owned: (REO) A term frequently used by lending institution as applied to ownership of real property acquired for investment or as a result of foreclosure.

Real Estate Settlement Procedures Act: (RESPA) A Federal law that requires lenders to provide home mortgage borrowers with information about known or estimated settlement costs.

Real Property: Land and appurtenances, including anything of a permanent nature such as structures, trees, minerals, and the interest, benefits, and inherent rights thereof.

Realtor: A real estate broker or an associate who holds active membership in a local real estate board that is affiliated with the National Association of Realtors.

Rescission: The cancellation or annulment of a transaction or contract by the operation of a law or by mutual consent.

Recorder: The public official who keeps records of transactions that affects real property in the area.

Recording: The recording in the registrar's office of the details of a properly executed legal document, such as a deed, a mortgage note, a satisfaction of mortgage, or an extension of mortgage, thereby making it a part of the public record.

Refinance: The process of the same mortgagor paying off one loan with the proceeds from another loan.

Rehabilitation Mortgage: A mortgage created to cover the costs of repairing, improving, and sometimes acquiring an existing property.

Remaining Balance: The amount of principal that has not yet been repaid.

Remaining Term: The original amortization term minus the number of payments that have been applied.

Repayment Plan: An arrangement made to repay delinquent installments or advances. Lenders' formal repayment plans are called "relief provisions."

Replacement Reserve Fund: A fund set aside for replacement of common property in a condominium, PUD, or cooperative project -- particularly that which has a short life expectancy, such as carpeting, furniture, etc.

Restrictive Covenants: Private restrictions limiting the use of real property. Restrictive covenants are created by deed and may "run with the land," binding all subsequent purchasers of the land, or may be "personal" and binding only between the original seller and buyer. The determination whether a covenant runs with the land or is personal is governed by the language of the covenant, the intent of the parties, and the law in the State where the land is situated. Restrictive covenants that run with the land are encumbrances and may affect the value and marketability of title. Restrictive covenants may limit the density of buildings per acre, regulate size, style or price range of buildings to be erected, or prevent particular businesses from operating or minority groups from owning or occupying homes in a given area. (This latter discriminatory covenant is unconstitutional and has been declared unenforceable by the U.S. Supreme Court.)

Revolving Liability: A credit arrangement, such as a credit card, that allows a customer to borrow against a pre-approved line of credit when purchasing goods and services. The borrower is billed for the amount that is actually borrowed plus any interest due.

Right of First Refusal: A provision in an agreement that requires the owner of a property to give another party the first opportunity to purchase or lease the property before he or she offers it for sale or lease to others.

Right of Ingress or Egress: The right to enter or leave designated premises.

Right of Survivorship: In joint tenancy, the right of survivors to acquire the interest of a deceased joint tenant.

- S -

Second Mortgage: A mortgage that has rights that are subordinate to the rights of the first mortgage holders.

Secondary Mortgage Market: The buying and selling of existing mortgages.

Seller-Provided Funds: Also called "Seller Contributions." Seller-provided funds include all transaction cost paid by the seller except the real estate agent's (or brokers) fee.

Servicer: The party who has entered into an agreement with the insured to service a loan.

Settlement Costs: See Closing Costs.

Single Premium: A premium, which provides coverage for more than a year.

Special Assessments: A special tax imposed on property, individual lots or all property in the immediate area, for road construction, sidewalks, sewers, streetlights, etc.

Special Lien: A lien that binds a specified piece of property, unlike a general lien, which is levied against all one's assets. It creates a right to retain something of value belonging to another person as compensation for labor, material, or money expended in that person's behalf. In some localities it is called "particular" lien or "specific" lien. (See Lien.)

Special Warranty Deed: A deed in which the grantor conveys title to the grantee and agrees to protect the grantee against title defects or claims asserted by the grantor and those persons whose right to assert a claim against the title arose during the period the grantor held title to the property. In a special warranty deed the grantor guarantees to the grantee that he has done nothing during the time he held title to the property which has, or which might in the future, impair the grantee's title.

Subprime Market: A term used to define higher risk borrowers. It usually consisted of borrowers that could not prove their income, had lower credit scores due to previous credit problems, or small down payments on high risk properties.

Survey: A map or plat made by a licensed surveyor showing the results of measuring the land with its elevations, improvements, boundaries, and its relationship to surrounding tracts of land. A survey is often required by the lender to assure him that a building is actually sited on the land according to its legal description.

- T -

Tax Lien: A claim against real estate for the amount of its unpaid taxes.

Teaser Rate: Similar to a Payment Discount, but implies either an unusually large initial rate discount or an attempt by the lender to lure an otherwise unqualified borrower into the mortgage.

Tenancy by the Entirety: A type of joint tenancy of property that provides right of survivorship and is available only to a husband and wife. Contrast with tenancy in common.

Tenancy in Common: A type of joint tenancy in a property without right of survivorship. Contrast with tenancy by the entirety and with joint tenancy.

Title: As generally used, the rights of ownership and possession of particular property. In real estate usage, title may refer to the instruments or documents by which a right of ownership is established (title documents), or it may refer to the ownership interest one has in the real estate.

Title Company: A company that specializes in examining and insuring titles to real estate.

Title Insurance: Protects lenders or homeowners against loss of their interest in property due to legal defects in title. Title insurance may be issued to a "mortgagee's title policy." Insurance benefits will be paid only to the "named insured" in the title policy, so it is important that an owner purchase an "owner's title policy", if he desires the protection of title insurance.

Title Search or Examination: A check of the title records, generally at the local courthouse, to make sure the buyer is purchasing a house from the legal owner and there are no liens, overdue special assessments, or other claims or outstanding restrictive covenants filed in the record, which would adversely affect the marketability or value of title.

Total Debt Ratio: Monthly debt and housing payments divided by gross monthly income. Also known as Back-End Ratio.

Total Expense Ratio: Total obligations as a percentage of gross monthly income. The total expense ratio includes monthly housing expenses plus other monthly debts.

Trade Equity: Equity that results from a property purchaser giving his or her existing property (or an asset other than real estate) as trade as all or part of the down payment for the property that is being purchased.

Transfer Tax: State or local tax payable when title passes from one owner to another.

Treasury Index: An index that is used to determine interest rate changes for certain adjustable-rate mortgage (ARM) plans.

Trustee: A party who is given legal responsibility to hold property in the best interest of or "for the benefit of" another. The trustee is one placed in a position of responsibility for another, a responsibility enforceable in a court of law.

Truth-In-Lending: (TIL) A federal law that requires lenders to fully disclose, in writing, the terms and conditions of a mortgage, including the APR and other charges.

Truth-in-Lending Disclosure Statement: A form required by federal law for lenders to provide to you full written disclosure on the mortgage loan amount being financed, fees and charges, the payment schedule, the interest rate, the annual percentage rate, and any other costs associated with the mortgage loan.

Two-to-four-family Property: A property that consists of a structure that provides living space (dwelling units) for two to four families, although ownership of the structure is evidenced by a single deed.

- U -

Underwriting: The process of evaluating a loan application to determine the risk involved for the lender. Underwriting involves an analysis of the borrower's creditworthiness and the quality of the property itself.

Universal Residential Loan Application: The standard mortgage loan application that is provided to a lender when applying for a mortgage loan. Also, know as a FNMA 1003 or FHLMC 65 form.

Unsecured Loan: A loan that is not backed by collateral.

- V -

Vested: Having the right to use a portion of a fund such as an individual retirement fund.

Department of Veterans Affairs (VA): An agency of the federal government that guarantees residential mortgages made to eligible veterans of the military services. The guarantee protects the lender against loss and thus encourages lenders to make mortgages to veterans.

- W -

- X -

- Y -

- Z -

Zoning Ordinances: The acts of an authorized local government establishing building codes, and setting forth.

About the Author

Karen Simpson-Hankins has been called "a go-to mortgage and real estate expert" in the media and a "breath of fresh air" by her clients. A 37-year veteran of the mortgage industry, author, coach and speaker, Hankins is undeniably a consumer's trusted advocate in home finance. Over her career, Hankins has focused on acquiring the best possible loan she could deliver at the best possible price for every client that crossed her path. Now, she also works with consumers around the country as an advocate to help them garner a better deal on every home purchase or refinance.

In 2012, Hankins became host of the weekly syndicated radio show, Surviving the Credit Crisis. Here, she helps inform consumers on a variety of topics related to the home buying and loan process. Her goal is simple—to help buyers feel less overwhelmed and vulnerable by arming them with valuable information that saves them thousands over the life of their loan.

Hankins grew up in central Oregon and has always been a numbers girl! She began by studying and working at a very early age in accounting, tax preparation and banking, before settling into mortgages, which turned out to be her life passion. She works every day to change consumer's lives and make their home-ownership dreams come true. She is a certified life coach, member of the SPAA and the International Association of Coaching, as well as her local area Chamber of Commerce, Tri-County Women in Business, licensed broker in Oregon, and a volunteer at her local church.

She currently lives in Oregon with her two children.

If you are interested in learning more information on home finance, tune in weekly to Karen's live radio show: *Surviving the Credit Crisis* or purchase the *Conquer Your Closing* Companion Workbook through her website at

http://www.karensimpsonhankins.com

You can also download her free guide, ***How to Outsmart Your Mortgage Lender and Save Thousands: 9 Critical Questions to Ask*** at

http://www.karensimpsonhankins.com/guide/

Connect with Karen on Facebook at
http://www.facebook.com/NeedMortgageInfoNow

and on Twitter at
https://twitter.com/ksimpsonhankins

or via email at
karen@karensimpsonhankins.com

32916885R00084

Made in the USA
Charleston, SC
28 August 2014